CD-ROM Included

PICTURE YOURSELF

CREATING
VIDEO GAMES

Jason Darby

COURSE TECHNOLOGY
CENGAGE Learning™

Picture Yourself Creating Video Games
Jason Darby

**Publisher and General Manager,
Course Technology PTR:** Stacy L. Hiquet

Associate Director of Marketing: Sarah Panella

Manager of Editorial Services: Heather Talbot

Marketing Manager: Jordan Casey

Acquisitions Editor: Heather Hurley

Project Editor: Sandy Doell

Technical Reviewer: Joshua Smith

PTR Editorial Services Coordinator: Erin Johnson

Interior Layout: Shawn Morningstar

Cover Designer: Mike Tanamachi

CD-ROM Producer: Brandon Penticuff

Indexer: Sharon Shock

Proofreader: Andy Saff

Printed in the United States of America
1 2 3 4 5 6 7 11 10 09 08

For product information and technology assistance, contact us at

**Cengage Learning Customer and Sales Support,
1-800-354-9706**

For permission to use material from this text or product, submit all requests online at
cengage.com/permissions

Further permissions questions can be emailed to
permissionrequest@cengage.com

The Games Factory 2 is the property of Clickteam.

Library of Congress Control Number: 2008902388
ISBN-13: 978-1-59863-551-5
ISBN-10: 1-59863-551-4

Course Technology
25 Thomson Place
Boston, MA 02210
USA

Cengage Learning is a leading provider of customized learning solutions with office locations around the globe, including Singapore, the United Kingdom, Australia, Mexico, Brazil, and Japan. Locate your local office at:
international.cengage.com/region

Cengage Learning products are represented in Canada by Nelson Education, Ltd.

For your lifelong learning solutions, visit **courseptr.com**
Visit our corporate website at **cengage.com**

To my wife Alicia and children,
Jared, Kimberley, and Lucas,
who support me in anything that I do.

Acknowledgments

CREATING A BOOK REQUIRES THE HELP OF MANY DIFFERENT PEOPLE and resources. There are a number of people without whom this book could not have been completed, and I would like to thank them all.

Many thanks go to the team at Course Technology PTR, who, as always, were efficient, friendly, and helpful in getting this project off the ground and doing all of the hard work of editing the book.

Thanks to Yves and Francois, the creators of The Games Factory, who made an easy-to-use product that makes the whole game creation process simple for anyone. I am also grateful for their prompt responses whenever I had a question. Thanks to Jeff Vance, who provided support through this process.

A hello and thanks go to Adam Lobacz, who used his excellent artistic talent to draw the storyboards in Chapter 3.

Thanks to my wife and children, who supported another book project, even though they know how much work is involved. Jared, Kimberley, and Lucas, you are the best kids a dad can have!

Thanks to everyone who reads this book, and anyone who has read my other books.

About the Author

JASON DARBY IS THE DIRECTOR OF CASTLE SOFTWARE LTD, an indie games and multimedia development company in the heart of the United Kingdom. Jason started on his computer creation business in 1998 when he released an offline web browser program. Since then, he has been working on projects for businesses, including a CD-ROM project for *PC Format Magazine* (UK), a number of quiz programs for large blue chip companies, educational multimedia programs, and small games.

Jason has had several books published in the Games Creation market, including *Make Amazing Games in Minutes*, *Awesome Game Creation*, and *Game Creation for Teens*. He has also published a book for people who want to make their own multimedia programs, called *Power User's Guide to Windows Development*.

Over the last few years, Jason has written several magazine articles in leading UK magazines, on game and screensaver creation. He has been published in magazines such as *PC Format*, *PC Gamer*, and *PC Answers*.

If you have any comments about this book, or would like to contact Jason about a general question, you can email him at jason@makeamazing.com.

Table of Contents

Introduction

THIS BOOK IS FOR PEOPLE WHO ARE INTERESTED in creating their own computer games for the Windows platform. Using the easy but powerful The Games Factory 2 software, you will be able to make games quicker and easier than ever before, without any programming knowledge.

Game creation is a lot of fun and easier than you might have previously imagined; it really is simple to start making your own games. The Games Factory 2 software that we use in this book allows you to make many different types of games, such as card games, board games, puzzles, platform games, side-scrolling games, shoot 'em ups, adventure games, and more. If you have always dreamed of making your own games, now is your chance.

Remember to try out different things and experiment with what you have created in each chapter before proceeding on to the next one. You will find this really is a lot of fun, but it's useful to take your time and learn about the product.

Assumptions

This is a beginner's book, and it is aimed at developers who want to learn the basics of game creation and how to make their own games. You do not need to know any programming languages, and as long as you have basic PC usage skills (can use the mouse and keyboard and navigate in Windows), you will be fine. Or you may be experienced in games programming or game creation and simply be looking for a book on The Games Factory 2; if so, this book is for you too.

Book Structure

The book is divided into 12 chapters and 2 appendixes. We begin with a straightforward discussion about the equipment you will need to begin making games. We then discuss how to plan your games, creating diagrams of how they will work. We then go through the basics of the program we use in this book, The Games Factory 2. In later chapters, we show you how to build games using the product.

By the end of the book, you should have enough knowledge to begin making your own simple games.

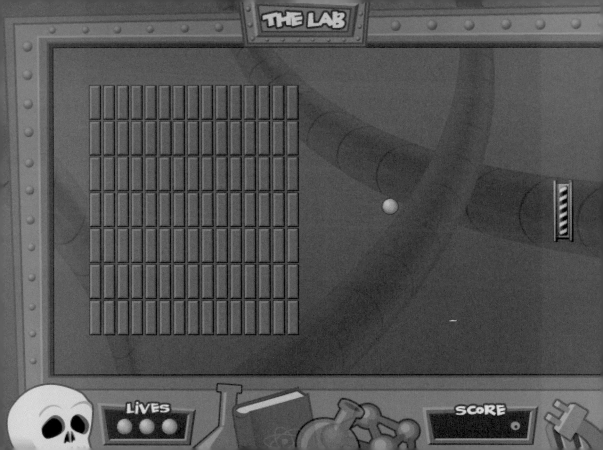

Starting Out in Video
Game Creation

CREATING COMPUTER GAMES has long been considered a difficult but rewarding hobby or career. Knowing where to start, which language to choose, and what hardware and software to buy meant that it was a potential minefield of disappointment and expense. Many people want to make games, but few know where and how they should start. You may have already tried to make a start but have come to an impasse and don't know what to do next.

In this first chapter you will learn which software and hardware you need. You'll also learn about some equipment that is just nice to have but not essential. You don't need much to get started, and most of the key items are things you probably already own. Throughout this book, we will use a game development creation program called The Games Factory 2; a trial version of this program is included on the CD-ROM with this book.

More information about The Games Factory 2 can be found at www.clickteam.com.

Games Creation Software

THE GAMES FACTORY 2 is the software that we will be using in this book to make our games. This is the key software needed to begin making your games. The software on the CD-ROM of this book allows you to make and save your games in its own native format. You will not be able to create a Windows-executable file and will need the full version if you want to create games your friends can play.

The Games Factory 2 (TGF2) allows anyone with just a basic computer game knowledge to be able to put together a game in a matter of minutes or hours. Rather than using traditional programming methods, where you would type in some text, compile it, check for errors, fix any problems, and then run your code again, TGF2 is an all visual creation program. You create or import your images and drag and drop them onto an area to create your scene. You then program your game logic using a graphical event system. The event system allows you to code your games using menus and selecting items from a menu.

Even though TGF2 isn't as powerful as traditional programming languages such as C++, it allows you to get results very quickly and still create commercial-quality games. The Games Factory 2:

▶ **Allows you to make games without the need to learn a programming language.**

▶ **Is inexpensive (a free trial version is included on the CD-ROM that accompanies this book).**

▶ **Is easy to use and easy to learn.**

▶ **Shortens development time and shows your results immediately.**

Insert Figure 1.1
A high-quality game made in TGF2 by 3dlight-studio.com for Castle Software Ltd.
© *3dlight and Castle Software Ltd.*

Hardware

YOU WILL NEED THE FOLLOWING equipment before you can begin making computer games.

Personal Computer

To use computer software, you obviously need a PC. The Games Factory 2 program is Windows-based, so you will also need a Windows operating system to run it. Although the Games Factory 2 software runs on relatively low specification computer hardware, the more memory, disk space, and processing power your computer has, the better. You can see the minimum and recommended specifications for installing and running TGF2 in the following lists.

Minimum Requirements
for Games Factory 2

- ► Operating System: Windows 98 Second Edition, Windows NT4 with Service Pack 3 or above, Windows 2000, Windows XP, Windows Vista

- ► Pentium Processer

- ► 32MB RAM with Windows 9x, 64MB with Windows NT, 128MB with Windows 2000 and Windows XP, 512MB RAM for Windows Vista

- ► CD-ROM drive

- ► Graphics card with 16MB or more

- ► Sound card (optional but recommended)

- ► 50–100MB free hard disk space

System Requirements

- ► Operating System: Windows 98 Second Edition, Windows 2000, Windows XP, Windows Vista

- ► Pentium 4 Processer

- ► 64MB RAM with Windows 98, 256MB with Windows 2000 and XP, 1GB RAM for Windows Vista

- ► Graphics card with 32MB RAM

- ► Sound Card

- ► 150–200MB free hard disk space

About PC Specifications

Determining the PC requirements for game making is not an exact science. Each game you make could be different and have differing amounts of images, sounds, and complexity. The more files you import and save to the hard drive, the bigger the game, the more complicated the game, the harder your PC will need to work. The more games you make and the more complicated they are, the more you will demand of your PC and the sooner you will want to upgrade.

Printer

A printer is a useful piece of equipment for printing out any documentation or information you want to review. There are many different makes and types of printers, some with built-in memory card readers. Others have integrated fax or scanning. You don't have to have a printer to be able to make games, but when you are doing the planning of your games, you may find it useful to print out your work. Printing out documentation makes it easier to review multiple documents at the same time. Sometimes trying to view several documents onscreen at once can be distracting or difficult.

Figure 1.2
A printer with a built-in scanner.

Paperless Office

When the PC came to be in common use many years ago, it was predicted that the paperless office would appear. This meant that no one would need to use paper any more. Many people still like to work looking at printed paper rather than onscreen a page at a time. Your preferences will determine whether you need a printer or not.

Scanner

If you are good at line art or drawing/sketching on paper you may want a scanner to get your drawings into a digital format. You will then be able to load them into a drawing package where you can add color and complete them. There is a great range in the quality of image different scanners can import, but many have a high enough import quality that the quality of your drawings won't suffer after import. If you already have a printer and scanner combination, this fulfills the requirement to do both while taking up half the space. A scanner is not an essential piece of your game creation kit unless you do drawing.

Digital Camera

If you wish to get photo art into your games, you have several options: you could purchase photos online, buy a photo CD, or use a digital camera to take your own photos and then import them. There are many devices that can be used to make images these days: webcams, mobile phones, and the traditional digital cameras, to name a few. Each type has varying scales of quality. Webcams are usually low quality; mobile phones are getting better with each new module, but they lack storage space; and digital cameras are relatively cheap, provide quality images, and can be had for less than $150.

You can make games without a digital camera as long as your games will not involve photo-realistic scenes.

Figure 1.3
A digital camera.

Joystick

Many games for the PC platform can be played with a joystick. When making your own games, you may want to have equipment that is likely to be used by people playing your games. The joystick is a perfect example of this. If you have made it possible for a user to play your game with a joystick, then you should test the game yourself with a joystick. Any game you make might play differently with different controllers, so it is a useful exercise to test your game using anything that will be allowed to the player.

Modem and DSL

Access to the Internet is an important aspect of any game creator's arsenal. You may have a high-speed DSL or a cable connection or still be using the much slower analog telephone system with a 56k modem. Whichever method you use, the Internet is a great way to research game ideas, look at demos for other games, or just obtain knowledge about a particular subject matter.

CD-Based Media

When you are making games, it is a good idea to back up your game files on a regular basis so that if you have any computer hardware problems, particularly hard disk failure, all of your game data will be safe.

In addition to CD-R, there are many different CD-based writing devices, including CD-RW, DVD-R, Dual Layer, and Blu-Ray. It doesn't really matter which type you have as long as it can save your games. The smallest size drive is around 720MB, which should be a good starting point for backing up your games.

Figure 1.4
Different media for CD and DVD.

CD-R Availability

The majority of PCs purchased today will have some form of CD writer already built into them, so you will most likely have access to one already. If you don't, you can pick up a CD-R device for less than $40.

Graphics Tablet

Rather than using a mouse to draw your computer graphics, which can be alien to anyone who is accustomed to drawing with a pen and paper, you may want to consider a graphics tablet. The graphics tablet provides a touch-sensitive board where you use a pen that operates in a similar way to a mouse. Many tablets also provide varying degrees of touch sensitivity, so the harder you press down, the more virtual ink will be applied in your paint package.

Dual Monitors

You have at least one monitor with your PC, but you might be wondering what the benefits would be of having two of them in your game creation setup. The reason for having two monitors is that when using Windows XP or Vista, you have the ability to place programs on either monitor at the same time. This allows you to view two different programs at any one time, rather than having to switch back and forth between programs.

When using programs like TGF2, you will want to utilize at least one screen for making your games, while you use the other screen for programs such as chat, browsing the Internet, or finding files. Once you have a dual monitor setup you will never want to go back to a single monitor configuration again.

Dual monitors are very useful for faster and more enjoyable working, but they are not essential for game making, so if you cannot afford another, or just don't have the space, this is not a problem. You can see a dual monitor setup in Figure 1.5.

Dual Monitors and Graphics Cards

To use the dual monitor facility on Windows, you will need a graphics card that has two video connections. If your card does not have a second video port, you will not be able to connect two monitors to it. You could upgrade your graphics card, or if you have the right type of PC, you may be able to put an additional graphics card into your machine and run the second monitor off that. If you are in any doubt, always seek the help of a PC professional before buying any equipment.

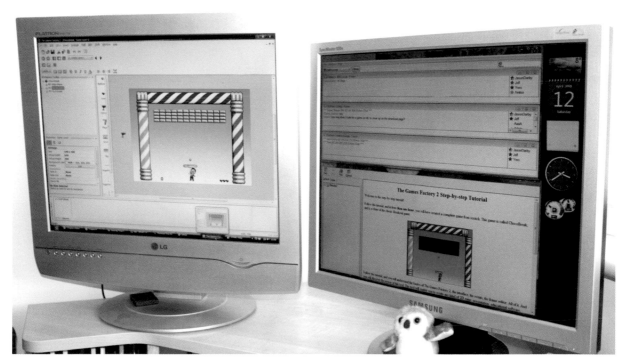

Figure 1.5
Dual monitors in use on a single PC.

Life:

Health:

Bombs:

3 X

Score:

0

Game Design

BEFORE WE BEGIN LEARNING about the Games Factory 2 software that is included on the CD-ROM, it is a good idea to think about any games that you would like to make. Then document what is going to happen and what is involved in the game before actually getting started on such things as graphics and programming.

How you think about your game and document it will ultimately help you in your goal of creating a game. Many people decide to make a game, but some fall into a common trap and try to make the ultimate game as soon as they have installed any software rather than first learning the basics. In some cases, this just leads to disappointment because the game you have always dreamed of making seems even farther away from completion than ever.

In this chapter, we will look at how to best document your game ideas. We will use the game we will create in Chapter 8 as our inspiration. We will be recreating the tutorial game called ChocoBreak, and using our storyboards and documents as a guide, we will create the game and then add additional levels and features.

So let's make a start on our game creating journey.

Product Design and Planning

YOU PROBABLY WANT to jump right into making your games, and who can blame you? Making games is great fun. But before you start, you should consider documenting what you intend to make. This will make your whole game making process a lot easier, and it will allow you to make games faster in the long run.

It doesn't matter if you are going to be making a game for your friends or family or considering a game that you might want to upload to the Internet for many people to try; it is always a good idea to write your game ideas down.

There are no right and wrong answers for creating game design documents for yourself, and any of the following concepts can be tailored to meet your own needs. As long as you are comfortable with what you are documenting and it is helping you to complete your game, you can pick and choose what you want to use from this chapter in your games.

Small Games

If your game is very small and will only take about 20 minutes to make, you probably don't need to write anything down; then again, it couldn't hurt and might make the creation go more smoothly in the long run. You should always use this process when you are making larger games. For smaller games, just consider it an option.

A basic structure of the order in which you do things can be seen in Figure 2.1.

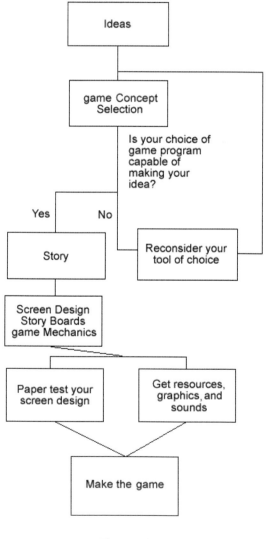

Figure 2.1
An approach to game design.

Your Ideas

THE BEST PLACE TO START IS with your game ideas. In fact, it's most likely that you will have many ideas for games and want to make as many of them as quickly as possible. The fact is you are better off selecting a single game idea as the game you want to make, because if you try to make a number of games at once, you will most likely not finish many of them.

Because you probably have lots of ideas floating around in your head, it is best to put them on paper where you can easily keep track of them all. It is easy to forget good game ideas, so by writing them down, you have at least a chance of remembering what they were about. The best way to write your initial ideas down is to put them into a simple list as shown in Table 2.1.

Table 2.1 Organizing Your Game Ideas

Game Type	Idea	Technology Concept	Rating	Difficulty
Bat and Ball game	You are on a break, a chocolate break. Time to get eating as much chocolate as possible. Using a player as a bat and a ball, hit the bricks to destroy them and score points.	Bat and Ball game, destroy the bricks, static levels.	High	Easy
Space game	You are the only surviving space space pilot from the academy. You now have to fight alone to save your planet.	Space Shoot-em up game—will include scrolling.	Medium	Medium
Scrolling	Aliens have invaded a small town in your local area. You cannot stand by watching impending disaster. A small team armed with weapons goes in search of the alien menace.	Scrolling—character-based game.	Low	Medium

Smaller Projects

It is a good idea to start making small games before jumping into larger games, as this is a good way to learn the game development tool. Smaller games are easier to complete than larger games, and if you are attempting to make a portfolio of games for professional use, small games show off your talents just as well as large games.

Creating the list will allow you to write down every idea you have. Don't worry about it if you are writing down game ideas that you think might not be very good; they might be the source of inspiration for another, better game months from now. You might be able to use some ideas as items in other games too, so don't worry if half your list consists of games you will probably never make.

Multiple Game Ideas

If you have a number of game ideas with the same rating, use the difficulty and technology columns to make it clearer which game you should make first.

Table 2.1 is split into five columns, explained in the following list:

▶ **Game Type: Categorize your game into a specific genre or type of game, such as Space, Scrolling, or Platform.**

▶ **Idea: Add a brief idea of what the game is about, or the aim of the player. This doesn't need to be very detailed, just enough information for you to remember what the object of gameplay is.**

▶ **Technology Concept: What things will the game need to include with regards to technology? Will it be in 2D, a first-person shooter, or require scrolling? Keeping a record of the technology required will allow you to track game ideas that you have the tools and software available to make now. It will also allow you to figure out which games you will have to put on hold until either your skills are at the right level or you have purchased a specific tool to meet a need of the game.**

▶ **Rating. How interested are you in making the game idea that you have? In your game making ideas, you will have games that you really want to make and those that are just an idea that you have yet to fully develop. Giving the games a rating will allow you to gauge which games you really want to pursue at this time.**

▶ **Difficulty: How difficult is the game idea you want to make? If the game is really complex, this difficulty rating will give you enough information to stay away from certain games until you have the necessary skills.**

The Story

Once you have selected the game you want to make, you may feel that you need to expand on your story a little more. If the game idea is small, you may not need to. It is impossible to be unique with regards to stories these days because many different ideas and concepts could be claimed as coming from one particular genre or idea. This doesn't mean that you should be taking other people's stories and using them in your own games, but it means your general concept isn't necessarily going to be new. For example, how many films and books can you think of that include zombies? Probably quite a few, but each one has a different plot or story-line.

The key to your story is to find the reason that the player wants to play the game. Is it to rescue someone or find a particular item? Did something happen to the characters to make them want to find or chase someone else?

Simple games don't need to have a large, complicated story. You can explain what the player needs to know in a paragraph. If you look at many of the games hosted on www.madword.com, you will notice that the accompanying story is only a few sentences. This is because the games themselves are fun and simple; they don't need long introductions and complex storylines. Think about your audience and how complex your game is before writing your story. If the game is a single level where the player does one simple task, a page worth of story is too much. Players don't want to read text or view the long introductory stories; they want to play your game.

The story to the game that we are making in Chapter 8 is as follows:

You love chocolate. It's 3:00 p.m. and it's time for your ChocoBreak. Eat as much chocolate as you can by destroying the chocolate bricks. Try not to let the ball disappear from the bottom of the screen or your break time will be over.

Keeping this short story in mind, we can now expand on what we want in our game. Following is a list of items or rules that we will want in our ChocoBreak game.

▶ **A selection of bricks. (These could be different flavored.)**

▶ **A number of lives.**

▶ **20 points for each brick destroyed.**

▶ **A menu screen to allow the player to navigate to the game.**

▶ **A high scores table that will display the top 10 scores in the game.**

▶ **An area of the screen (top, left, right) protected so the ball does not fly out in that direction.**

▶ **A ball that will bounce on hitting the top, left, and right objects as well as the player's bat.**

▶ **Music playing on main screen and high score screen.**

▶ **Different sounds when the ball hits various objects.**

▶ **The player to be controlled by the mouse.**

From this list, we can now think about how our game is structured screen-wise and begin to think about our storyboards.

Storyboarding

OW THAT YOU HAVE AN idea what you want in your game, you can start to draw it out on paper. This is called storyboarding, and the process is used to give you an idea what your game will look like before you start to draw graphics and place your items onscreen.

TGF2 works on the basis of frames, where each level and screen is a different frame, which makes the whole process of mapping out our ChocoBreak game very easy.

There are a number of different storyboarding drawings you can do at various levels of your game. Following is a sample of drawings you might make for your storyboard:

▶ **Game Map: This is the top view of all of your screens and levels. This is a simple and effective way of seeing how all your levels connect together, giving you an overall view of how the user will navigate around the screens in your game. You can see an example of a game map in Figure 2.2. This is our structure for the ChocoBreak game, where we will have three screens. You can use several letter-sized pieces of paper stuck together or a single piece to create your map; it all depends on the size of your game.**

▶ **Level or Screen Map: In Figure 2.2 you can see the individual screens but not the actual content that you are hoping to place within them. So at this point, you should break your game down further into additional storyboards for each screen. You can see our three-frame game, ChocoBreak, broken down into further storyboards in Figures 2.3, 2.4, and 2.5.**

▶ **Object Level: It is very common in more complex games to storyboard an individual object, such as a player character or enemy spaceship. Here you would draw the individual object, and on the same document, detail additional notes about that particular object. So if you were detailing the player character, and he has changeable clothes or armor, you wouldn't necessarily detail each item. You would just mention what is interchangeable with the character.**

Paper, Paper, Everywhere

When you are creating a large game, it is sensible to label all of your drawings so that you know where they fit within the game. You may end up spending a lot of time thinking about where all the levels go if you do not document and label your work correctly.

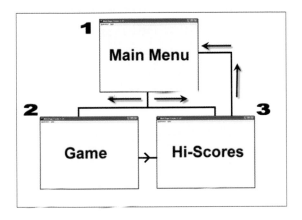

Insert Figure 2.2
The game map for ChocoBreak.

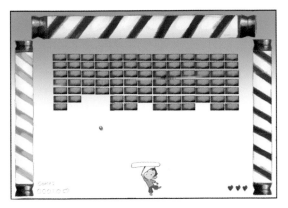

Figure 2.4
Our game storyboard for the ChocoBreak game.

Drawings and Text

Storyboarding doesn't just involve drawing pictures; the pictures can also have particular text on each drawing to give more detail or make a concept or interaction more clear.

Figure 2.5
Our end screen storyboard for the ChocoBreak game.

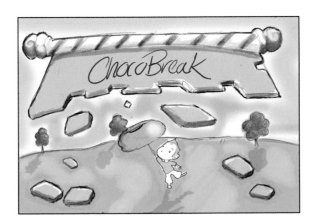

Figure 2.3
Our main menu storyboard for the ChocoBreak game.

Storyboards Using Computer Graphics

If you are not very artistic, you might worry about drawing storyboards. Another option is to use default graphics that you can download free from the Internet or find on the full version CD-ROM. This way, you can still create a basic storyboard without having to worry about your artistic skills. This is particularly helpful if you are preparing a storyboard for artists and want to give them a good idea what you want.

Getting to Know
The Games Factory

YOU PICTURE YOURSELF WANTING to be a game creator, either for fun or maybe even as a career of some kind. You have the hardware available. and you have the trial software of The Games Factory 2. You are now ready to make a start on your game making journey.

You might have some reservations at this point because game creation could mean getting into programming and difficult-to-learn concepts, but don't worry. The Games Factory 2 is a straightforward product to learn.

In this chapter, we will learn all about how to navigate the product. We'll also take some step-by-step walkthroughs of certain functionality that will help you later on when you make your own games. Finally, you will also learn the location of the program editors and what they are used for.

Making games is within your reach, so keep reading and before you know it, you will be creating your first game.

The Games Factory 2 Program Introduction

THE GAMES FACTORY 2 is a powerful but easy-to-use programming system that allows anyone, even those with no programming knowledge, to make games and screensavers. As with any creation system or program, you must get to know its interface so that you can get around quickly but also get to feel comfortable using it. TGF2 only has a few screens and editors so once you have gotten acquainted with it, you don't need to use the program regularly to remember what to do when you come back to it.

Remembering Traditional Programming

Traditional programming languages can be difficult to remember when you're just starting out in your game making life. Many are based on typing in code and having specific words that you need to type (syntax). You won't have this problem with TGF2 because it is all mouse-led. Once you have learned the basics, it won't matter if you take a break from the program for a while. You'll have no problem getting back into creating when you start again, because you won't need to remember specific syntax or code.

In The Games Factory 2 program there are three key program creation editors, one picture editor, and a special calculator for entering special information. The editors and programs are as follows:

▶ **Storyboard Editor:** Lets you specify the order of screens or levels within your game. Each level or screen is called a frame. You can create as many frames as you like within your TGF2 program.

▶ **Frame Editor:** Here, you look at a specific frame and place the graphics and objects onto the screen. You could consider this the area where you set the scene of your game.

▶ **Event Editor:** Here is where you create your program login in a spreadsheet-like program. You create events, which tell TGF2 how to react in the game.

▶ **Picture Editor:** The Picture Editor is where you can draw, import, and export images. It has another editor built into it called the Animation Editor. This is so you can create multiple pictures of the same image and animate it, so that it looks like it is moving within your game.

▶ **Expression Evaluator:** When you need to do calculations and comparisons of numbers or text, or obtain information, you will use the Expression Evaluator. It looks like a giant scientific calculator with some extra buttons on it.

Launching The Games Factory 2

W E ARE NOW READY TO start up TGF2 and take a look at its interface. The following assumes you have installed the program demo from the CD-ROM included with this book, which is stored in the Demos folder.

You can either double left click on The Games Factory 2 icon that will be on the desktop or choose Start > All Programs > The Games Factory 2 > The Games Factory 2. One of two things will happen:

▶ **In the demo version (included with the CD-ROM in this book), you will see a dialog box which will advise you that it is the demo version, as shown in Figure 3.1. You can click on the Continue button to move to the main screen.**

▶ **In the full version you will move to the main interface screen.**

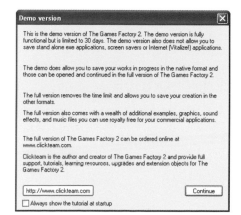

Figure 3.1
The trial version dialog.

You will now see The Games Factory 2 program screen load, and you will see an HTML help tutorial program open on the right side of the screen, as shown in Figure 3.2.

We will be creating a simple game using the tutorials graphics later on in this book, but for now you can close the Tutorial window by clicking on the Red X in the top right corner.

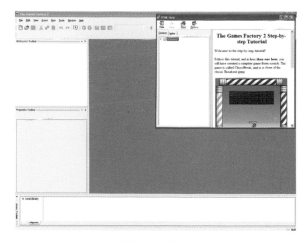

Figure 3.2
The TGF2 interface and an HTML tutorial file.

ChocoBreak Tutorial

The ChocoBreak tutorial was made for TGF2 by Olivier Behr, and you can visit his web site at http://www.oliverpearl.com. The ChocoBreak game is a classic type of game that was very popular on computer systems during the 1980s.

Introducing The Games Factory 2

THE MAIN GAMES Factory 2 interface allows you to access all of the key components in one simple interface area. It has different buttons, tabs, and windows to learn.

After a short time spent getting to know the basics, these other options and features won't delay your game creation creativity. As you get more experienced, you will then be able to use these additional shortcuts and features to make your games even quicker. You can see the main windows of TGF2 in Figure 3.3.

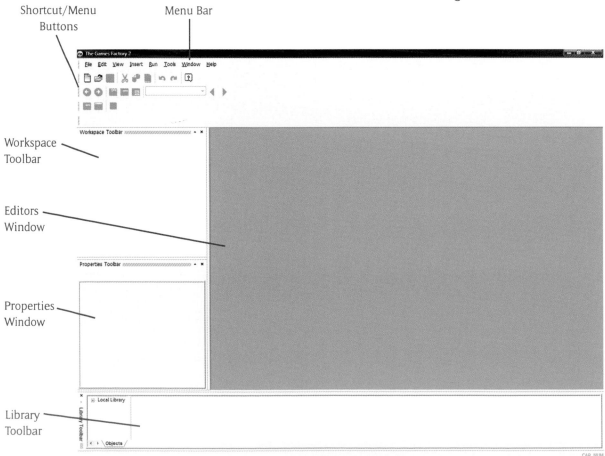

Figure 3.3
The layout of TGF2.

Menu Bar

The menu bar is a standard way of accessing specific features within any Windows-based application, and TGF2 is no exception. When you select one of the options from the menu at the top, it will display a popup menu, which displays all of the options under that heading. If you see an arrow next to any of the options in the list, this means that it is a subheading and has more items under it. You can see that the File option has been selected in Figure 3.4.

In some of the options, you will notice keyboard options like Ctrl+N. These are shortcut keys, so you can use the key combination to do the same choice with keys rather than navigating through the menu.

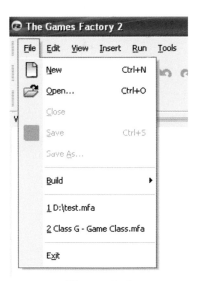

Figure 3.4
The File menu.

Shortcut Buttons

The shortcut buttons reside at the top of the application window and are a short list of all the important options available in the program. These buttons will change at different times, depending on what you are doing and which editor is currently displayed. You can see a close-up of the shortcut buttons in Figure 3.5. You will notice that many of the options are grayed out; this means that they are not currently available.

Workspace Toolbar

When you create your applications, the Workspace toolbar will display the physical folder and file structure of your game. You can see an example of the structure involved in the Workspace toolbar in Figure 3.6. At the very top of the structure, you will see the application name. Below the application name you will see any frames that are within this game. Within each frame, you will see the objects that you are using for that frame.

Frames are physical separations of your game within the program, so these may be multiple levels or screens where you want to display something. A perfect example of this would be that shown in Figure 3.6. There you see a menu screen that displays a loading screen, which either tells the player a story or displays a waiting screen before the game begins. The second frame is the game screen, where the player will play the game, and the final frame is the end screen, which gives the player the score or end sequence to the game.

Figure 3.5
The shortcut buttons.

Objects are the games assets, such as graphical items, objects to handle the score, lives, and so forth. Without objects, you would not have anything displayed onscreen. A perfect example of this is the Active object, which is used for any objects that will move or be animated onscreen. This is used for game objects, such as spaceships or meteorites. In gaming terms, the Active object could be considered a game sprite.

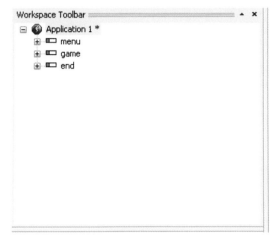

Figure 3.6
A game loaded into the Workspace toolbar.

Levels and Frames

Even though we have made the distinction of placing one level on each frame, you can make many levels on a single frame. The upside of this is that you only have to place the graphics on a single frame rather than duplicate them over many frames. The downside is that it can get very messy on a single frame if you create 50 or 100 levels with different graphics.

Properties Window

Many items within the TGF2 program can have a set of properties assigned to them. These properties allow for fine-tuning of that part of the program. You can configure many aspects of the program using properties, and you would normally do this before beginning any event programming. You can see an example of the Properties window in use in Figure 3.7.

Figure 3.7
The properties of a particular application.

The levels of property configuration are:

- ▶ **Application Level Properties: Any changes to the application level of properties will affect the whole application. These can include information, such as the size of the program window, whether the window will have maximize or minimize buttons, any help file the program will include, and copyright information.**

- ▶ **Frame Level Properties: Any changes will only affect the frame that they are made on. You can have many frames, and you may want some of them to react differently. You can do things such as sizing frames, fading in and out of a frame, grabbing the desktop, and changing the background color.**

- ▶ **Object Level Properties: On each of your frames, you drop items called objects, and each of these objects can have a set of properties, such as movement, size, screen location, and any special information that might be stored in it.**

Editors Window

You will notice on Figure 3.3 that there is nothing displayed. This is because at the start of any creation, no editors are open. Within this gray background will appear the editors that we have previously mentioned.

Library Toolbar

The Library toolbar is a way of accessing graphic and object content. Clickteam, the maker of TGF2, has provided a large set of game backgrounds, buttons, animations, and characters to use in your games. This means you can use the product straight out of the box rather than having to draw or import your own content. If you are using the trial version on the CD-ROM that comes with this book, you will be provided with a set of graphics for the tutorial game. We also have provided some additional graphics to get you started making your own fun games. These can be found under the \Content directory on the CD-ROM.

When you are using the Library toolbar, you navigate a number of folders and files and then, once you find something you are interested in, you drag and drop this to your frame. You can see the Library toolbar in use in Figure 3.8.

The Library Toolbar Visibility

You may not initially see the Library toolbar. To switch it on and off, you can use the menu bar and select View > Toolbars > Library Window.

Figure 3.8
The Library toolbar in use.

Layers Toolbar

The Layers toolbar is not displayed by default and not shown in Figure 3.3. When you want to place graphics at different layers, you can either do so on the frame or via the Layers toolbar. A layer can be thought of as the layers of a cake; some parts are on top of others. You can only see parts of certain layers depending on how much the layer above it covers the layer below it. For example, if you eat half of the top layer of a cake, you will see part of the layer below it revealed. The same applies to layers in a game; you might have a graphic partly covering another, and it will appear in front of the graphic below it. If you use art packages, you will be familiar with layers. You can see the Layers toolbar in Figure 3.9.

Layers Visibility

To switch on the Layers toolbar, you will use the menu bar, then select View > Toolbars > Layers Toolbar.

Figure 3.9
The Layers toolbar.

The Games Factory 2 File Basics

BEFORE WE GET DEEPER into The Games Factory 2 software, we will need to take a look at the creation of a new application and the loading of a file that has already been worked on. Many of the features of TGF2 will not appear unless there is a game file loaded. Let's take a quick look at opening, saving, closing, and creating a game file.

Creating a New TGF2 Game File

Before you can start making your games, you will first need to create a blank game file. This blank file will contain a basic set of property information and a single game frame for you to begin working on.

To create a new file, complete the following steps:

1. Load up TGF2, by double clicking on the icon on the desktop, or by clicking Start > All programs > The Games Factory 2 > The Games Factory 2.

2. Click on the New button, press the Ctrl+N keys, or use the File > New menu option.

Once you have created your new blank application file, your game is ready to be put together. You can see the blank application in Figure 3.10.

Application Files

A game, and all its contents, that is made in TGF2 is called an application file.

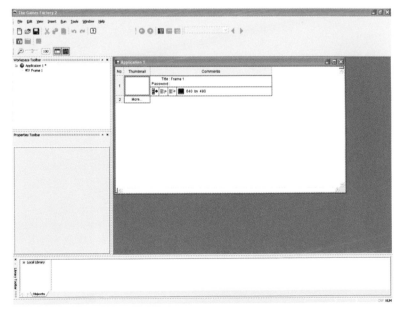

Figure 3.10
The blank application file with a single frame and the Storyboard Editor open.

Opening an Existing Game File

If you have a game that you have previously created or have perhaps downloaded a game from the Internet that you want to open, there are two ways to do this.

▶ **Browse your machine using Windows Explorer until you have located a file with an MFA extension (this is a file that ends with .mfa). Double left click on it, and it will automatically load into The Games Factory. Even if you don't have TGF2 already started, it will make it appear and then load the file into it.**

▶ **If you already have TGF2 open and know where the MFA file is located, you can click on the Open button and use the shortcut Ctrl+O or click File > Open on the menu. You will then get a browse dialog box as shown in Figure 3.11. You can then browse for the file, single left click on it to select it, and then click on the Open button to load the file.**

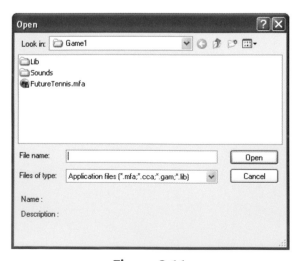

Figure 3.11
The browse dialog used to find MFA files.

File Extensions

Files that are created in TGF2 are saved as name.mfa, name being the name that you call your game. This is a file that can be opened on any computer that has TGF2 installed on it. If you own the full version of TGF2, you will also be able to save files in EXE format. This is a finished version of your game, which cannot be opened by TGF2.

Saving a Game File

You have begun to create your game and you want to save the file for reloading later on. You may also want to save the game file to ensure having a backup file just in case of any problems. You should try to back up your game files on a regular basis just in case there is a power loss or computer crash, which could damage the file you are working on.

To save a file, you can do one of the following:

▶ **If this is the first time you have saved this file, click on the Save button, use Ctrl+S, or use the menu to select File > Save As. A dialog box will appear. Type in the name of the file you wish your application to have. Click on the Save button to save the file.**

▶ **If this isn't the first time you have saved this file and you wish to stay with the same file name, you can use the Save button, press Ctrl+S, or click on the File > Save option.**

The Editors

W̲E BRIEFLY MENTIONED THE editors that are used in TGF2 earlier in this chapter. We will now be taking a closer look at them and how to access them. These editors are parts of the program that you will use the most and by the end of the book, you will be very familiar with them. There are three main editors for constructing your games: the Storyboard Editor, the Frame Editor, and the Event Editor.

You can quickly and easily move among these three editors by using the buttons on the menu. You can see the button graphics for the three editors in Figure 3.12.

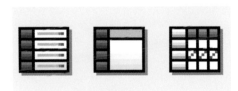

Figure 3.12
The Storyboard Editor, the Frame Editor, and Event Editor buttons.

The Editor Buttons' Appearance

Not all editor buttons will be available at all times.

Storyboard Editor

Most games are composed of several levels, or screens. The Storyboard Editor lets you view all of your frames in a list. This makes it easy for you to see the order of the frames, and you can drag and drop frames above or below others. You also get a visual representation of each frame's contents in a small thumbnail image so if you don't remember exactly what a particular frame contains, you might remember from the picture. You can see an example of the Storyboard Editor with a number of frames added in Figure 3.13.

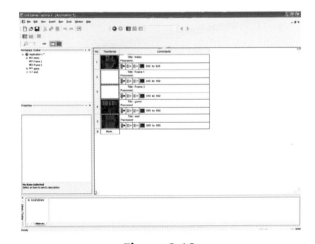

Figure 3.13
The Storyboard Editor with a number of frames loaded.

Storyboard Options

Some other options available in the Storyboard Editor include setting the size of each individual frame, setting a frame name, and creating a fade in and out transition effect.

Creating Frames

When you make your own games, you will need to create a set of frames that will hold your game's content, such as the game's graphics. These frames can be the levels in your game or the different screens the player will visit. You may create as few or as many as you require for your game. To create new frames, you can use one of the following methods:

First Method:

1. Start TGF2.

2. Create a new application by pressing the New button or selecting File>New from the menu. This will create a single frame application file.

3. Click on the number 2 in the Storyboard Editor. This is the number that is opposite the text More.

4. Adding one will increase the last number, which is opposite the More text. Continue to click the number opposite the text More to continue adding the number of frames you require.

Second Method:

1. Start TGF2.

2. Create a new application.

3. Right click on the application name in the Workspace toolbar. From the popup menu, select New Frame.

4. Continue right clicking and selecting New Frame to create the number of frames you need.

Renaming Frames

You will notice that when you create a frame it will have the name of Frame with a number at the end of it. Every time you create a frame, it will increase this frame number. When creating a large game, you will find this numbering system is not very helpful, especially when you tell TGF2 to jump to a specific frame, and you are required to select that specific frame. This is not such a problem when you only have three frames and you know what each frame does. You might create a game with a large number of frames, and remembering what each does by number would be very difficult or impossible. Renaming them to something more appropriate can help a lot with this, because you could specify that a frame fulfills a particular role within your game, for example, Level 39 or End Screen.

In the same way that there are two ways to create frames, there are also a number of ways to rename a frame.

The first method is:

1. You have your TGF2 program open, with an application created or open.

2. Right click on the frame number text in the Workspace toolbar and select Rename from the popup menu.

3. The frame you choose to rename will now allow you to type in the text of the frame. You can see the before and after results in Figure 3.14. You can see in the example that the Frame 2 text has been changed to Game.

The second method to change the frame name is:

1. You need to ensure that the Storyboard Editor is open. Then single left click on the Title text (under the comments) for the particular frame that you want to rename.

2. Type in the name of your frame and press Enter.

3. You can see the before and after results of the name change using this method in Figure 3.15. In the example, you can see that the title of Frame 1 has been changed to Menu.

Figure 3.14
Editing and renaming the frame names.

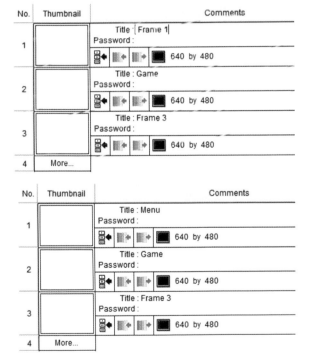

Figure 3.15
Changing the frame name using the Storyboard Editor.

The Frame Editor

The Frame editor, as shown in Figure 3.16, is the blank starting slate of your frame. The Frame Editor is where you place your game graphics and the objects that you need to make your game work. The white area in the middle is called the play area. This is the window that will appear when you play the game and is considered the viewable area of the game. The gray area surrounding the play area is where you can place items that you do not want to have initially appear at the start of your game. You could say that the Frame Editor is where you set the scene of your game.

To give you an idea of what the frame could look like in a working game, see Figure 3.17 as an example of a game being set up on the frame.

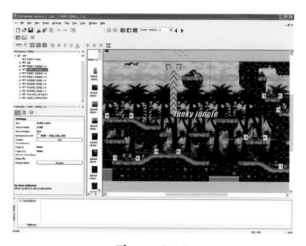

Figure 3.17
A complex game loaded in TGF2 and displayed in the Frame Editor.

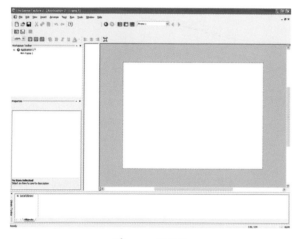

Figure 3.16
All new frames will appear as a blank white area.

The Event Editor

This is the screen where you build the logic of your game. You could say this is where you do your programming. The programming is based on *eventing*, which is an English-readable form of programming based on checking for each event for conditions. If the conditions are true, then the appropriate actions occur. There is an Event Editor for each frame of the game, so if you have a three-frame game and you program something for the first frame, you will not see this information in the second or third frames. You can see an example of the blank Event Editor in Figure 3.18 and one with code applied in Figure 3.19.

What Are Events?

Think about your everyday life, and consider what an event is. An event could be going to work, making a cup of tea, and going to bed. An event is not a single item, but a combination of items. For example, making a cup of tea involves filling the kettle with water, switching it on, waiting for it to boil, and so on. In TGF2, an event is a collection of items called conditions.

What Are Conditions?

A condition in TGF2 checks to determine when a specific task is true. If the condition (or conditions) is true, the program will run the actions. If we take making a cup of tea, a condition for this could be "has the kettle finished boiling?" If this is correct, then the condition is true. In TGF2, it works the same way: "Is the score set to a specific amount?" "Is the player's character at a particular position on the screen?" "How many lives does the player have?"

What Are Actions?

An action is something you want to happen. So if a certain condition is true, you would run the relevant actions. An example of this could be that the player's spaceship has been hit by a missile, in which case the action might be to reduce the ship's health or to subtract a life. You can have multiple actions as the result of a particular event.

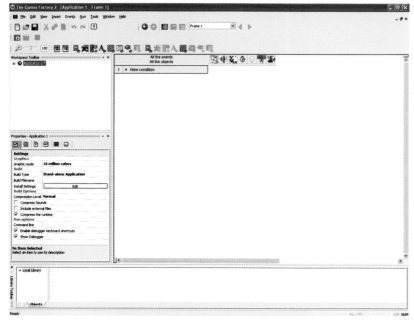

Figure 3.18
The blank Event Editor.

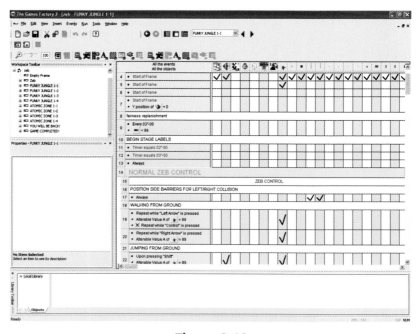

Figure 3.19
The Event Editor which has been programmed.

The Picture and Animation Editor

Throughout this book, we will refer to the Picture and Animation Editor as the Picture Editor, although it is actually two editors in one. Whenever you are dealing with objects that are of a graphical nature, you may with to edit them, or you may even want to import graphics of your own. To do this, you will need the Picture Editor. If you wish to animate a graphic, in other words, make it appear to be moving, waving, or rotating, you will need to use the Animation Editor. This editor appears in the bottom half of the Picture Editor. You can see the Picture Editor in Figure 3.20. We will cover more about the Picture Editor in Chapter 6.

Animation Versus Movement

You may think that animation is the same as movement, but this is not the case. Movement is the physical moving of an object (graphical or otherwise) on the screen. Animation is changing the look of an object's state. This could be making a character wave his arm, or a spaceship tilt to the left or right. By combining the two options, you can create some amazing looking game graphics.

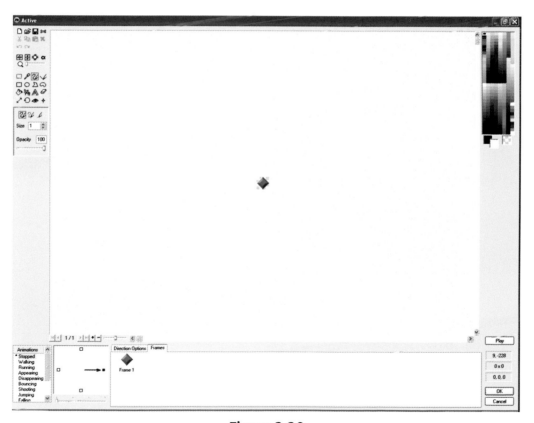

Figure 3.20
The Picture Editor with the Animation Editor in the bottom of the screen.

The Expression Evaluator

When using the Event Editor or the Frame Editor, you may be required to test and compare numbers or text or get information from another object. The Expression Evaluator looks like a large scientific calculator, and it is used to type in specific data that you want to retrieve from the program or its objects. You will use the Expression Evaluator most when using the Event Editor. You can see an example of the Expression Evaluator with some information entered into it in Figure 3.21.

Objects Contain Information

All objects contain information, for example, their position onscreen or their size. They can also contain additional information, data (called alterable variables), which you can read and write to. This information is all accessible from the Expression Evaluator.

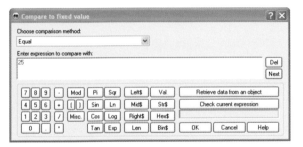

Figure 3.21
The Expression Evaluator in use.

Getting Help

ALTHOUGH THIS BOOK will give you a lot of information on how to make your own games with The Games Factory 2, you will at some point need more help to allow you to understand a specific concept or find out about a particular feature.

There are a number of different help options available to you if you have gotten stuck on a particular problem. The first and quickest way to get help is to use the built-in help system. You can access the built-in help by using the menu option Help > Contents. You can see the help system in Figure 3.22.

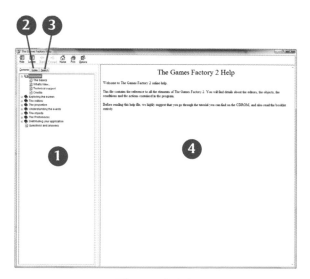

Figure 3.22
The built-in help system.

You can see several items in Figure 3.22 that correspond to the following numbered list:

1. By default, you will see the contents list. If you have used the help system before and used a different tab, this will be the default view. The contents show all of the different subject headings of the help system. You can click on the plus (+) sign to expand the contents and the minus (–) sign to collapse them.

2. The Index provides a list of all of the keywords that are used in the TGF2 help system. So, if you are looking for a particular item, you can type in the word and let the help system search for it. If the word you are searching for is a keyword, it will appear in the list in the left window and you will be able to click on an item to display its contents in the right window.

3. The Search tab allows you to do a more detailed search than the Index. The Index is only words that have been identified within the help system, while the Search tab will search all of the documents used in the help file and display the available content headings. It will also highlight the word in the contents as you look through them.

4. This is the content window, which displays the help file information.

Tutorial Files

Another way of learning how to do something or understanding particular concepts is to look at the various tutorial files that are available. By looking at them and seeing how they are structured and the code that they use, you can learn a great deal. You can also pick the code apart and use similar code in your own programs. Tutorial files are a very easy way of learning new things.

Tutorial Files

With the trial version of TGF2, the program has a single tutorial file. We have included a number of games so that you can look at the source code to see how they are structured. In the full version of TGF2, there are several games and example files for you to learn from.

Downloading from the Internet

Always be careful when downloading files from the Internet and ensure that you are using an anti-virus program which can check on anything that you intend to place on your PC's hard drive and open.

The Internet is also a great source of example files and tutorials. Clickteam's web site has a number of example files you can download as well as text-based articles, and you can find a lot of different code examples on the forum uploaded by its users. Other users also upload examples to their own web sites that you might find useful.

Running Your Games

WHEN MAKING YOUR GAMES, you will want to test them occasionally to make sure they work correctly or to see how you are getting on with your game. There are two ways to test your game. The first is to run the whole game; this will play the game from the very first screen (called frame) and allow you to play it until the game exits or you decide to close the program. The second method allows you to run the current frame you are on. This is a good way of testing the frame you are working on without needing to skip or play through all the levels that precede it.

You can see the Run Application and Run Frame buttons in Figure 3.23.

Figure 3.23
The Run Application and Run Frame buttons.

Shortcut Keys

You can also use shortcut keys to run the application or frame by using F7 (Run Frame) or F8 (Run Application).

Creating the Scene
and Using Objects

I N CHAPTER 3, WE TOOK A TOUR of the TGF2 program and had a look at its toolbars, menus, and editors. You should now be getting an idea of the workflow of TGF2 and how you would go about using it.

In this chapter, we will be looking at setting up a scene, placing the graphics and other objects onto our game frame. Setting your game scene is a major aspect of creating your game, and in many cases, you might be setting your scene based on your storyboards.

As well as placing your game graphics, you will also be placing other items called objects on the game frame. These objects are one of the most important aspects of creating your games with regards to setting up your scene and getting it ready to be programmed.

Objects in TGF2

OBJECTS COULD BE CONSIDERED the cornerstone of anything you create in TGF2. In fact, they could be considered the single most import thing required for your game. A game is comprised of various components, for example, a simple spaceship graphic, the graphic of a bullet being fired from an enemy creature, in-game video, onscreen text displaying your name, and an item that displays how many lives you have left. Anything that is added onto the frame is an object. The structure of these objects is already defined using a built-in list of objects that comes with TGF2.

The great thing about these objects is that they are pre-programmed, allowing you to get on with the task of making your game and then configuring the object in the way you want it to work. You will then be able to access most objects via the Event Editor, which allows for conditions and actions to be applied to them.

Adding an Object

To view all the available objects in TGF2, first you must be in the process of adding an object. You can only add an object if you are on the Frame Editor screen. You might have 10 frames in your game, and so you must be in the frame you want to add your objects.

Following are the steps to view and add objects to a single frame.

1. Start TGF2, and select File > New from the menu.

2. Double-click on the text "Frame 1" in the Workspace toolbar. This will load the frame into the editor area of the program.

3. You can now view and add an object using two methods: You can select Insert > New object from the menu, or you can right click on the blank white frame area and select Insert Object.

4. You will then see a list of available objects that you can choose from, as shown in Figure 4.1. You are also able to display the objects in a list by clicking on the tick box on the right side below the buttons. Select the object that you want to add by single left clicking on it and then clicking on OK.

5. You will be taken back to the frame, but your cursor will have changed to a cross. Left click on the frame to place the object.

More Objects

If you are running the full version of TGF2, you may see some additional objects. Clickteam sometimes adds additional objects via updates and patches.

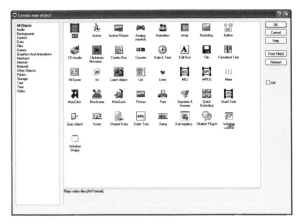

Figure 4.1
The Create new object dialog box.

Accessing Object Properties

Every object you add to the frame has a set of properties. These properties can be accessed by single left clicking on the object. These properties might include:

1. The object's screen location, using two coordinates of X, which is horizontal, and Y, which is vertical.

2. The object's size or angle on the frame.

3. Whether the object should be resized and if so, whether it should be resized using a speed algorithm or based on quality.

4. Whether the object should be transparent or use any ink effects to change the look of the object when the frame is run.

5. Whether the object should have any movement applied to it, and any additional movement configurations, such as speed, bounce, and rotation.

You can see the object Properties window shown in Figure 4.2. When accessing object Properties, you will see a set of tabs, which allow certain properties to be grouped together for ease of use. An example of the Properties tabs can be seen in Figure 4.3.

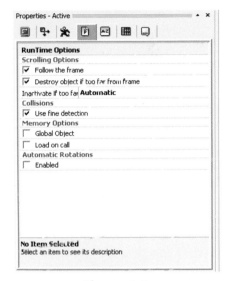

Figure 4.2
The object Properties of the Active object.

Figure 4.3
The tabs available on the Properties window.

Tabs Available

For different objects, there will be different tabs available in the object Properties window. Some objects will only allow very small changes to their properties.

An example of the types of tabs you will encounter are:

▶ **Display Options:** This provides different options for how the object should appear on the frame.

▶ **Size/Position:** Determines the object's size and position on the frame. This tab is used a lot to place an object at a specific location on the frame.

▶ **Movement:** Those objects that can have movement are set to static by default. You can specify a different movement type from within this tab.

▶ **Runtime Options:** Determines how the object should react when the program is running. This allows configuration of such things as when an object should be destroyed and if it should use specific collision properties.

▶ **Values:** You can assign different text and number values to an object, which are then available to program in the Event Editor.

▶ **Events:** You can create events that just apply to the object. You access a special event editor just for the objects.

▶ **About:** Provides information about the object, and a button link to the help file. If you click on the help file button, it will open the help file associated with the object or property you are currently viewing.

Tab Identification

You can identify the tabs by holding your mouse cursor over them; a small text box will appear telling you what each tab is.

Some objects have too much property information to store in the Properties window and will open a separate window on top of the Frame Editor window. To begin with, many of the properties will be fine for starting out, but later on, you may find that you have to edit these properties to make your game look and feel the way you want it to.

Common Objects

WE WILL NOW TAKE A LOOK at some of the common objects that you will use on a regular basis in your game creation. There are over 40 objects that come included with TGF2, which can do many things from displaying text to creating a quiz program. We will look at the key ones you will need when making simple computer games.

Active Objects

Active objects are used as the main graphics for your games and will probably be the most common objects that you will use. These graphic objects could be a spaceship, bullets that fire from a spaceship gun, a walking character, or a player item, such as bonus health or lives. The key reason for picking an Active object is that the graphic will move, rotate, or animate in some way.

Active Objects That Don't Move

You can also use active objects for graphics that will be static and not animated. Each type of object has different properties that can be applied to it, and you may find the active object is perfect for a specific task. You may also want to animate a graphic later on in the development of your game. This makes the whole process easier if you change your mind about an object and make it animated.

Active objects are denoted by their icon of a running man in the Create new object dialog box and as a green diamond in the Event Editor. The icons can be seen in Figures 4.4 and 4.5. You can access the Active object graphic by double left clicking on the green diamond. This would take you to the Picture Editor, where you could then make changes to it or import another image. We will cover the Picture Editor in Chapter 6.

Figure 4.4
The Active object icon.

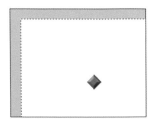

Figure 4.5
The default Active object inserted onto the frame.

Backdrop and Quick Backdrop Objects

Backdrop and Quick Backdrop objects perform a similar function, and that is to provide a background to your games. A Backdrop object is usually constructed by using the Picture Editor to import or draw an image; you could alternatively use one of the many backdrops provided on the CD-ROM of the full version of the software.

You use Backdrop objects to create a background for your games; for example, if you were making a space game, you might create a backdrop that has a planet and stars in it. Backdrops will always appear at the back of the frame, and you cannot place them on top of other objects.

You can see the icons for the backdrop and Quick Backdrop in Figure 4.6.

Backdrop   Quick Backdrop

Figure 4.6
The Backdrop and Quick Backdrop icons.

The Backdrop object uses an imported image, using the Picture Editor, but the Quick Backdrop object allows for further configuration to create a background of different types. To take a look at the specific properties of the Quick Backdrop object, we need to add the object onto the frame and then access its properties.

1. Ensure that TGF2 is started, and create a new application by clicking on the New button.

2. Double-click on Frame 1 to display the first Frame Editor. Right click on the frame and select Insert Object.

3. Select the Quick Backdrop object and click on OK.

4. Click on the Frame Editor to place the object.

You will now see the object properties and the tabs that are associated with the Quick Backdrop object. There are two areas of interest for anyone wanting to use this object for backgrounds. The first is under the Settings tab, under the headings of Shape and Type. The Shape allows you to change the general shape of the Backdrop object. The Type is more important as it changes the type of fill that the Quick Backdrop can use; you can see the settings in Figure 4.7.

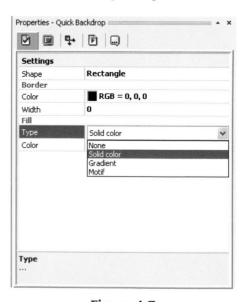

Figure 4.7
The Type drop down box with the possible options you can choose.

You have the following configurable options when using the Type drop down box:

▶ **None:** This creates a shape which is not filled, so, for example, if you select a rectangle, it will just have a black border by default.

▶ **Solid color:** This fills the shape with a color. You can change the color by clicking on the color settings property.

▶ **Gradient:** This creates a color that changes its shade, so that it changes from one color to another. If you have played old computer games, you might recognize the gradient option; it was very common in games in the 1980s to simulate backgrounds, especially those for a sky effect. You can see an example of a gradient in Figure 4.8. You can also see the properties that we have selected to make this happen in the Properties window.

▶ **Motif:** This option allows you to import an image and then display this image multiple times on the frame. You can see an example of this in Figure 4.9, where we have used an image as a motif.

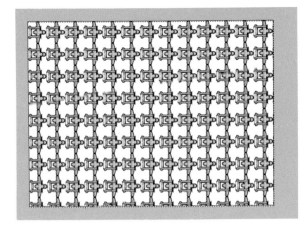

Figure 4.9
A fighter plane, replicated many times to create a motif.

There is one other major setting of the Backdrop and Quick Backdrop objects and this is kept under the Runtime Options tab. This is the Obstacle type as shown in Figure 4.10, and it determines how the object will interact with other objects and, in particular, the player's character. In total, there are four settings that you can choose from:

▶ **None:** This option means that the Backdrop object will not interact with any other objects on the frame and will be just a backdrop. This is the default setting and is used when you just want to display the background.

▶ **Obstacle:** This allows you to check for any collisions between the backdrop and any other objects. You can check for any collisions between an object and the backdrop in the Event Editor.

▶ **Platform:** This will allow the backdrop to take the form of a platform. A platform is a floor, upon which a player character or computer-controlled character can walk.

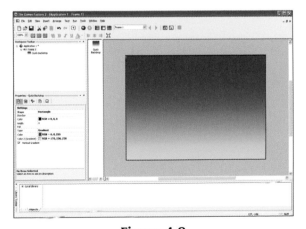

Figure 4.8
The gradient setting, set up as a rectangle and using two blue colors.

▶ **Ladder:** This will allow the backdrop to act like a ladder, so when the player presses the up key on the keyboard, the player's character graphic will move upwards and climb the ladder.

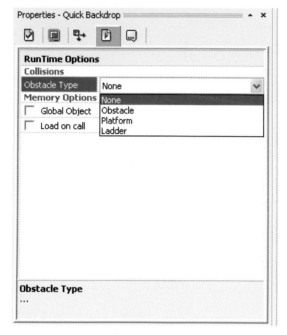

Figure 4.10
The Obstacle Type options in the Object properties window, the Runtime Options tab.

Button Object

In your games, you may want to create a button to allow the player to move between screens or get the user to make a selection from a group of options. TGF2 has a Button object, which allows you to configure the type of button you might want in your game. You can see the Button object icon that is displayed in the Insert Object dialog box in Figure 4.11 and the button that is placed on the frame in Figure 4.12.

Navigation

The Button object can be used as a key navigational aid for the player. It enables the player to get from one frame to another when she clicks on the button. In other cases, you will make the game move automatically between frames using other methods, such as time, score, or clicking on text.

Selection

You may want the player to select from a number of options. You can do this also with the Button object. This is useful if you have a game configuration screen where you get the user to pick how he wants the game to work or play.

Button

Figure 4.11
The Button object icon.

Figure 4.12
The Button object placed on the frame.

Default Button

The default button that is created by TGF2 is a Windows button. This is the standard type of button that you will see in Windows applications. This is not used often in games because it doesn't fit with a game's style.

There are five different options available for selecting different types of buttons in your games. Having a wide range of button types is useful. It means you can select a button type that matches your game rather than being stuck with a default-only option. These options are shown in Figure 4.13 and are described in the following list:

▶ **Text Push button:** This is the default option and is a standard Windows button you might see in PC applications such as an FTP server, a screensaver, or an e-mail program. You can see a standard button in Figure 4.12.

▶ **Checkbox:** The checkbox is another useful Windows button type, which allows the player to click on a button and tick it. This is called a checkbox and you can have a single checkbox or many of them, and allow the player to switch some on or off. You can see an example of the checkbox in use in Figure 4.14.

▶ **Radio button:** The radio button is another selection button. You can choose to display one or a number of radio buttons. The difference between this and the checkbox is that you use the checkbox when the user can select multiple options, while the radio button is used when they can only select one from a group of radio buttons. You can see an example of the radio button in use in Figure 4.15.

▶ **Bitmap Push button:** With the Bitmap Push button, you are able to import your own images to use for the button, meaning you can design an image that fits in with your game. The Bitmap Push button allows for three states: normal, pushed, and disabled. For each one of these states, you create a different image. You can see an example of the normal and clicked states in Figure 4.16.

▶ **Text and Image Push button:** The final button is similar to the Bitmap Push button, has three states, but also allows the developer to add text, to the left, right, above, or below the image. You can see an example of this in Figure 4.17.

Five Button Properties

As each of the five buttons is different in some way, they all have different properties. These settings may determine what font to use to display the text or how an image might be created and displayed.

Figure 4.13
The Type settings in the object properties for the button object.

Figure 4.14
An example of a set of checkboxes which allows for multiple selections.

Figure 4.15
An example of a radio button which allows for a single selection within a group of buttons.

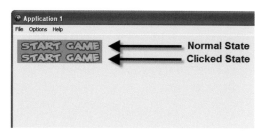

Figure 4.16
An example of a Push button with two states displayed graphically.

Figure 4.17
An example of a Text and Image Push button, with the button above the text.

Hi-Score Object

When you want to display a hi-score table in your game, you can use the Hi-score object. Unlike a traditional programming language, where you would have to program each line of the table, TGF2 has already set this up for you. All you need to do is configure how you want it to look. By default, the hi-score table displays 10 names and score entries, and it will automatically check to see if a hi-score is generated by the player. If so, it would then ask the player for her name and then enter it into the table. You can see the icon for the hi-score table in Figure 4.18 and the default look of the table in Figure 4.19.

Hi-Score

Figure 4.18

The Hi-score object icon.

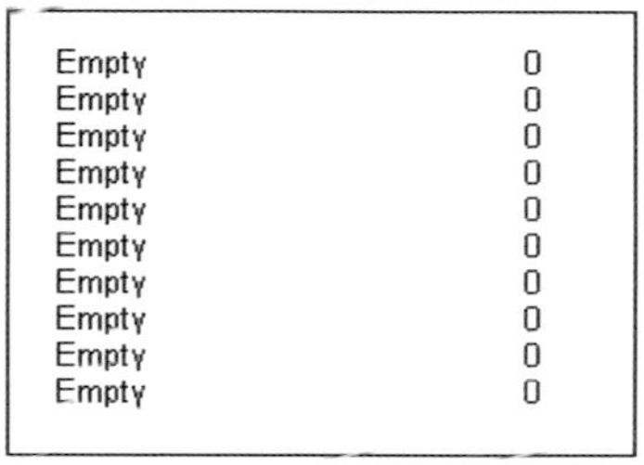

Empty	0
Empty	0
Empty	0
Empty	0
Empty	0
Empty	0
Empty	0
Empty	0
Empty	0
Empty	0

Figure 4.19

The default scoreboard.

Hi-Score Generation

The TGF2 program knows when a hi-score is generated, so you don't have to program it. It has a list of the default scores that are displayed within the Hi-score object. When the player enters the frame that contains the Hi-score object, it will compare the player's score with those in the table. You can also configure it so that it doesn't check for a hi-score by default.

Arcade Games from the 1980s

In older computer games and arcade machines from the 1980s, you might be asked for only three characters for your name.

You have a number of configurable options available to you in the object properties, particularly in the Settings tab, which can be seen in Figure 4.20.

▶ **Number of scores:** The number of scores that you want to display in your table. The default listing displays 10. If you have a small area in which to show scores, you can reduce this figure.

▶ **Length of names:** You can configure the number of characters that the user is able to use for his name once he gets a high score.

▶ **Show name before score:** You can switch the name and score around to display either one first.

▶ **Hide at start:** This will enable or disable the visibility of the hi-score table when the frame is run.

▶ **Check at start:** This is enabled by default and will check to see if there is a hi-score and then present the player with a box to enter his name.

▶ **Hide scores:** If you do not wish to display the scores, but just the names, you can enable this option.

▶ **Edit content:** This allows you to amend the default starting names and scores for your game. You can see the setup box in Figure 4.21.

▶ **Name (Ini file to use):** By default, the scores are saved on the user's computer in a file called cncscore.ini. If you want to create a different ini file to save the information to, you can enter the file name in this box.

Multiple Hi-Score Tables

If you want to have a number of separate hi-score tables within one game, you can create multiple ini files to store the information.

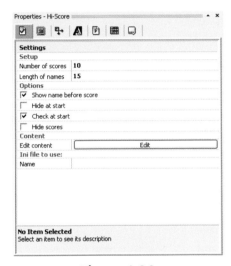

Figure 4.20
The Settings tab for the Hi-score object Properties window.

Figure 4.21
The dialog box for entering your own names and scores.

Text-Based Objects

In many games, you will want to add text on to the screen, maybe for instructions or comments or to tell the user the game is over. TGF2 can easily handle text using its collection of text objects. You can use the following three objects for adding text to your games:

▶ **Formatted text: The formatted text object allows you to display text but also import text from an RTF (rich text format) document. RTF is a common text document, used in Wordpad or Microsoft Word. You can open, save, and load an RTF document as well as print it. You can also make the window transparent, which is very useful if you want to display items behind the object.**

▶ **Static text: This is a very basic text object that does not interact with the frame in any way and is displayed on top of any objects. This object is not transparent, so is not very useful for a graphically busy screen.**

▶ **String: This simple text object can display text on the frame. You can create multiple paragraphs for this object and then select at runtime which paragraph to display; the object also is transparent.**

You can see the object icons in Figure 4.22.

Formatted Text   Static Text   String

Figure 4.22
The three text objects that you can use in TGF2.

Each of the three objects allows you to specify the size, font type, and styles of the text you will use in the object, but each of the three objects has various properties that are unique to each object. You can access the font options from the toolbar or from the object properties window. You can see the toolbar options in Figure 4.23.

Figure 4.23
The various font options available from the toolbar when using the text objects.

Lives

The Lives object allows you to keep track of how many lives a player has. You can then make decisions based on how many lives the player has left. For example, if the player has no lives left, you can tell the program to go to another frame or display a Game Over message. You can set, add to, and subtract from the Lives object.

You can see the Lives object icon in Figure 4.24 and how it is displayed on the frame in Figure 4.25. As you can see in Figure 4.25, it displays the lives as three heart graphics. This is because the initial starting value of the Lives object is 3.

Lives Graphics

If you don't like the heart graphic as your Lives image, you can change it by editing the properties and replacing the image with another, or you can draw your own.

Starting Lives

You can change the starting lives number by accessing the application properties Runtime tab. The Lives object will read the amount stored in the application level and then display the relevant number of heart images. If you change the application level number, this will amend the image on the frame.

Lives

Figure 4.24
The Lives object in the Object Selection dialog box.

Figure 4.25
The default display on the frame of the Lives object.

For the Lives object, you can access the graphic configuration of the object in the Settings tab of the object properties. You can see the settings in Figure 4.26. They consist of the following:

▶ **Player:** **This is the player to which the current Lives object will apply. You can have as many as four players in your game, so you can select which one this object applies to.**

▶ **Type:** **If you want to change the look of the lives, using an image, displaying it as text, or displaying it as a number.**

▶ **Images:** **By clicking on the Edit button, you can enter the Picture Editor and then replace the standard image used for the lives icon.**

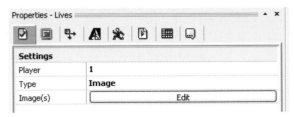

Figure 4.26
The Settings tab of the Lives Object Properties.

Score

Another essential game object is the Score object. The Score object is used to keep track of a player's current score. You are able to set the current value and then add to and deduct points from it. The Score object is a counter that stores a number.

You can see the Score object icon in Figure 4.27.

Score

Figure 4.27
The Score object icon in the Add Object dialog box.

Using the

Event Editor

THE AREA WHERE YOU WILL SPEND most of your time in the Games Factory 2 is the Event Editor. This is where you program the game logic and make your games come to life. The Event Editor is where you do your game programming, but unlike traditional programming, where you might type in lots of text and then get an error message, TGF2 is a wholly different experience. TGF2 is an all visual programming language, which means to start making games you use the mouse, and, yes, you will need to do some typing, but usually that's to add specific values.

In a traditional programming language, you might write some code, and when you are ready to run it to see if it works, the programming tool might give you an error message. You then have to go back into the code, find the error, and retest it. Hopefully, you will find the problem and it will run. This can be sometimes slow and laborious. TGF2 is different and gives immediate feedback and will never give you an error message of this kind. If you program something incorrectly, for instance, telling a bouncing ball to move left when you meant to tell it to move right, the error manifests itself onscreen, so that you can immediately see that you made a mistake and correct it. The great thing is that any programming errors you might make are visual and logical.

In this chapter, we are going to look at the structure of the Event Editor, how it works, and how you enter in your code and other information.

The Event Editor

To use the Event Editor, you will need to be on the frame that you wish to create your code against. Remember, each frame can have different events assigned to it, and the event sheet is unique to that frame. To access the Event Editor:

1. Create a new game file by clicking on the New button or by selecting File > New, or, alternatively, you can use the shortcut key of Ctrl+E.

2. Double-click on the Frame 1 name in the Workspace toolbar.

3. You will now see the blank frame. Click on the Event Editor button to access the blank frame.

The Event Editor is now ready for you to begin programming. There are a few things to note. First, you will notice seven icons across the top of the page as shown in Figure 5.1. These are called system objects and are always present within every Event Editor that you open.

As you add active, string, hi-score, and other objects to your frames, these will also appear in this list, as shown in Figure 5.2. This list of objects is called the Event Editor Object list.

Frame and Event Editor

When making your own games, you might have multiple frames, and you will certainly have objects already placed on the frame before accessing the Event Editor.

All the events All the objects	
1 • New condition	

Figure 5.1
The seven default objects that appear in every Event Editor.

All the events
All the objects

Figure 5.2
The seven default objects and others that have been added to the frame.

Object Icons in the Event Editor

There are two objects that will not appear in the Event Editor Object list; they are the Backdrop and Quick Backdrop objects. This is because these objects do not generally interact with any part of the game.

The System Objects

As previously mentioned, the first seven icons are reserved for system objects. These objects perform many of the basic tasks and functionality of a TGF2 game, from playing sounds to moving between frames. You will access these objects in two places: when you create a condition and when you create an action.

Conditions

In Chapter 3, we discussed conditions; remember, a condition occurs when you want to check for something.

Actions

In Chapter 3, we discussed actions; an action occurs when you want something to happen to a particular object.

 Special Conditions perform special functions, such as enabling and disabling groups, accessing the clipboard, creating loops, and accessing text or numbers.

 If you want to play sounds and music, you would use the Sound object. You can also use this object for checking when a sound has begun or finished playing.

 Storyboard Controls tell you which frame the game is currently on, and provides navigational commands, such as jump to frame, next, and previous frames. The Storyboard Controls object also controls the running of the application and can restart and close the application.

 If you want to measure an amount of time that has passed or check for something at a certain interval (every 5 seconds, for example), then you can use the Timer functions.

In many games you might want to create an exact copy of a game object, for example, an enemy space ship. The Create New Object function allows you to test for these objects and pick one at random, or to create new objects.

 You will use the mouse pointer and keyboard object if you want to check when the user has pressed a key, moved the mouse into a specific area of the screen, or pressed a mouse button. You can also hide or display the mouse cursor within the game using this object.

 The Player 1 object allows you to check the status of a player's lives and score as well as any controls the player might be using (joystick or keyboard). Using this object, you can check the number of lives or perhaps add or remove a life.

Events

Events are the names given to single or multiple conditions that have a common task; the events are the grouping of these conditions. Each event line is given a line number starting with the number 1. When you first access the blank event system, you will see a single line with the words New Condition; this is a blank event line waiting for you to begin programming.

The conditions within these events are tested by TGF2 when the game is run. When these conditions are true, the program will run that event line and the actions corresponding to that line. If they are currently false, they will be ignored and checked again once the program has been through all of the other events below it.

Different events may be true or false at different times during the life of the game. For example, you may have a condition/event that checks for when the player presses the spacebar. If the player does not press the spacebar, then this event will be false. Once the player presses the spacebar, it will be true, but after the actions have run, unless the player is still pressing the spacebar, the event will again be false.

Readable Code

Most code you enter in the event lines (the gray boxes) will be readable as it is displayed in English and is quite logical.

We will create our first event that will contain one condition; this condition will run when the frame has started. This is just an example of how to add an event, and the process for adding further single events is the same. The Start of Frame condition we will use is very useful for setting up certain conditions of your game before it starts.

▶ **Click on the New Condition text. This brings up the New Condition dialog box as shown in Figure 5.3.**

▶ **You will notice that the New Condition box contains the seven system objects. If you had added any further objects, they would be displayed here as well.**

▶ Right-click on the Storyboard Controls icon; this is the icon that looks like a chessboard and knight. A popup menu will appear which displays all the possible conditions that you can create for this object, as shown in Figure 5.4.

▶ Select the Start of Frame text from the menu.

▶ This will now add a single condition to our first event line, on event line 1, as shown in Figure 5.5.

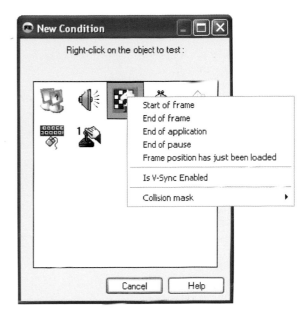

Figure 5.4
The popup menu from right-clicking an object.

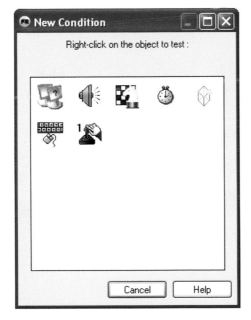

Figure 5.3
The New Condition dialog box.

You can add multiple conditions to the same event. This allows for more complex code statements; for example, you could add a condition that checks to see if the mouse cursor is over an object. The second condition could then be that the user presses the spacebar. TGF2 will only run this event if both conditions are true. This allows you to create quite complex statements and make your games much more fun and complicated, using the same simple Event Editor process.

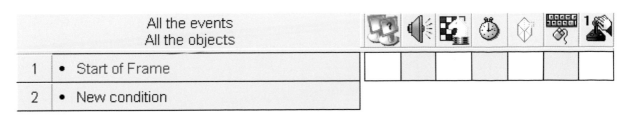

Figure 5.5
The single condition in event line 1.

To add a second condition to the same event you will need to:

▶ **Right-click on the Start of Frame text in the first event line. This will bring up a popup menu, as shown in Figure 5.6.**

▶ **Select Insert and you will then be presented with the Choose an Object dialog box. This allows you to insert a new condition with the one that has already been created.**

▶ **Select the Player 1 object, then right-click. From the popup menu, select When number of lives reaches 0.**

▶ **You will now have two conditions in one event line, where both conditions have to be true before TGF2 will run any actions.**

As previously mentioned, when the program is run, it will check this event and see if it is true. In the case of the example in Figure 5.7, the start of frame is always run when the frame is first run, so this is true immediately. The second condition is then checked to see if it is true. In this case, TGF2 will check to see if the player's number of lives equals 0. By default, the application lives is set to 3, so this second condition is false, and the event line will not run. TGF2 will now skip this line and continue to run any below it. At the moment, there are no more events.

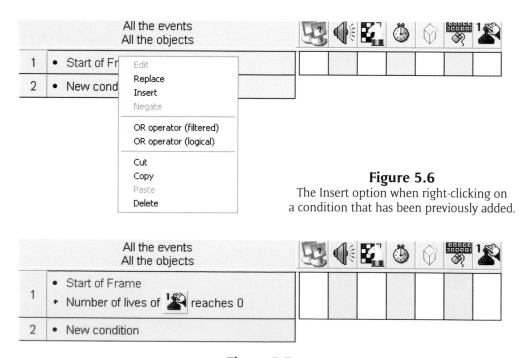

Figure 5.6
The Insert option when right-clicking on a condition that has been previously added.

Figure 5.7
The two conditions now entered into one event.

Start of Frame

The start of frame condition is only run when the frame starts. In the case of Figure 5.7, the second condition is not yet true, and even if the number of lives changes to 0 later on in the game, this event will no longer run because the start of frame condition will no longer be true.

Actions

An action is what you want to happen. We have already discussed the seven system objects and how any additional objects you add to the frame will appear. The action boxes are directly to the right of the events, in the blank white and gray squares. When you want to add an action, you will first find the event that you want to use the action on and then move across to the right until you are directly under the object you want the action to apply to.

In the event we have just added in Figure 5.7, perhaps we want to end the application if the number of lives equals 0. The action to end an application is under the Storyboard Controls

object, so from event line 1 we move across until we are directly under the Storyboard Controls object as shown in Figure 5.8. As you can see in Figure 5.8, we have highlighted the action box with a cross. To add an action, you would right-click this box. Once you right-click on an action box, you will get another popup menu. From the popup menu, you can select from any number of options, but choose End the Application.

You can see the popup menu options for the Storyboard Controls object in Figure 5.9.

You can add actions to any of the object in the object list on the same event line, and you can also add actions to the same object. All you will need to do is right click on the action box where you have already added an action in order to add a further action. You can add many actions on the same object.

When you have added an action, the action box displays a check icon as shown in Figure 5.10. This tells the programmer that something exists on this event line. To see what code is placed on this action box, you will need to hold the mouse over it, and a box will appear showing the code as shown in Figure 5.11.

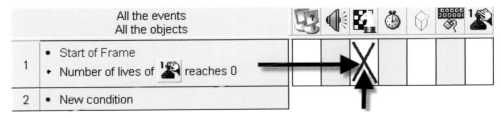

Figure 5.8
The location of the Storyboard action box on the first event line.

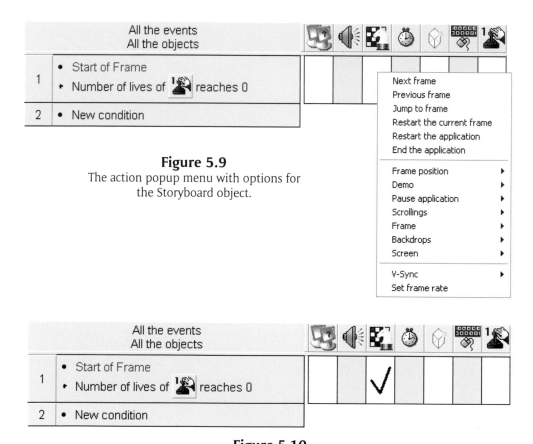

Figure 5.9
The action popup menu with options for the Storyboard object.

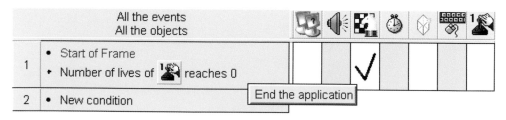

Figure 5.10
The action box displays a check when an action has been assigned.

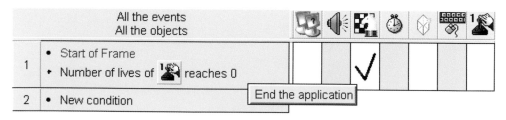

Figure 5.11
How to see the actions under an action box.

Comments

Comments are useful for a number of different reasons; it is always good to label your game with details such as when it was created, the date it was last amended, and any general comments about the game. This way, if you open up your program a long time after you created it, this information may provide an insight into when you made it and what it does.

Comments are also very useful for commenting your code. So if you write a particularly difficult piece of code, you can place some information between lines of code or at the start of the code to explain what you have done and how you achieved it. This is important if you leave your code for any amount of time and then go back to it, because it may take some time to familiarize yourself with what you have done. Adding comments makes this process a lot quicker, meaning you can get back to programming rather than spending time trying to understand what you have done.

To add a comment:

▶ **Right-click on an event line number. In the case of our single event line, you could do this on the number 1 or the number 2. Whichever line you do this on, the comment will appear above that line number.**

▶ **We intend to add a comment on the top of the Event Editor, so right-click on event line 1. A popup menu will appear. Select Insert > A Comment from the popup menu as shown in Figure 5.12.**

▶ **An Edit Text dialog box will appear as shown in Figure 5.13.**

▶ **Enter your text in the text area. You can also change the font, font color, and back color, as well as setting the alignment of the text.**

▶ **For the example shown in Figure 5.14, we have selected Centered text and typed in the words My First Program. We set the background color to a light red (the first red on the color picker). To complete the text comment, you need to click on OK.**

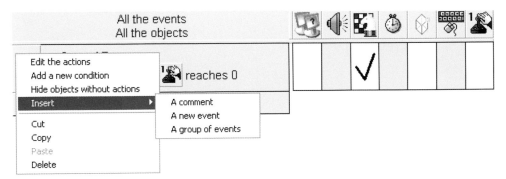

Figure 5.12
The popup menu when right-clicking on an event number.

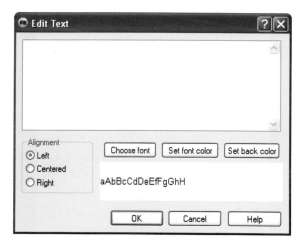

Figure 5.13
The Edit Text dialog box.

The Need for Comments

There is no requirement to add comments to your programs. In fact, you don't need to add any for your program to work. You may find that it will help you understand your programs when going back to them later, though. Even simple programs can benefit from adding comments.

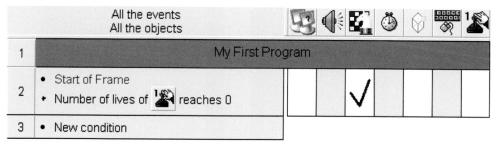

Figure 5.14
The final comment with the changes applied via the dialog box.

Code Groups

Creating events on lots of lines is something that you will do in every program, but sometimes you may find that you need to group a set of events together and keep it separate from the main set of code. As the program runs from top to bottom reading the conditions, you may want some code not to run until a specific point in time, but it would run if it was a normal event line. These two items can be corrected by creating a code group.

A code group allows you to tidy up your code by placing it in a group, which can be expanded or collapsed, and that helps keep the Event Editor tidier. Additionally, you can enable and disable a group, so that when the code is being run through by TGF2 it can be ignored until a point when you want this code to run.

To create a code group, you will need to access the event number popup as you did for creating a comment:

> ▶ **Right-click on any event line number. If you still have the example we have been working on, right-click on event line 3.**
>
> ▶ **A popup will appear. Select Insert > A Group of Events.**
>
> ▶ **A dialog box will appear, called Group Events, as shown in Figure 5.15.**
>
> ▶ **Enter the title of the group. In this case, we will call it First Group. You can password protect the group if you want, but in most cases you can leave this blank.**
>
> ▶ **You will notice that the Active when frame starts checkbox is checked. This is the default setting. To ensure that the code within this group does not run when the program is run, you must uncheck this.**
>
> ▶ **When you are happy with the group name, click on the OK button to create the group. You will see the created group in Figure 5.16.**

You will notice in the created group that there is an additional New Condition line. You can either create new events using this button or cut and paste code you've already written and place it in the group.

Enabling Code Groups

Code groups can be enabled and disabled using the Special Object in the Event Editor.

Figure 5.15
The code events group ready for configuring.

Drag and Drop

You can also drag and drop event lines into a group by clicking and holding down the left mouse button on the event line number and then dragging to the group line.

Figure 5.16
The final look of the code group added to the Event Editor.

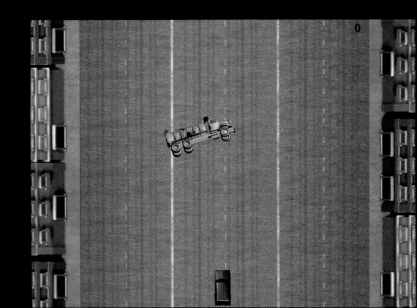

Movement

I N NEARLY EVERY COMPUTER GAME you will play, the graphic
characters, spaceships, and items will move on the screen. Movement
is a key component of making your game, and in this chapter we will
look at how we move things from one part of the screen to another and
how to let the player control the movement of an object.

Movement is an important part of making a game in TGF2. If we consider
the order in which a game is made, first would come setting the scene,
where you create your frames and place your objects. You next would
configure object properties and movement, and then you would program
the logic in the Event Editor. You might be wondering why this Movement
chapter falls after the Event Editor in Chapter 5, when it precedes it in
setting up a game. The reason for this is that although you would configure the movement properties before going into the Event Editor, in order
to really make some of your movements work correctly, you will need to
do some logic programming. You wouldn't have been able to do that
before learning about the Event Editor.

So we will now take a look at all of the movements available to our games.

Accessing Movement

I N CHAPTER 4, YOU LOOKED at all the available objects and added some of them to the frame. Nearly every object you can apply to the frame can have a movement assigned to it. Some objects generally do not require a movement in games, for example, the button object, but the option is there if you ever require it.

> ## Default Movement
>
> All objects by default are set to static movement.

Copy and Paste Objects

If you copy and paste objects from other games, they will retain the movement properties assigned to them.

To display an object's movement property, first we need to have an object on the frame. In this example, we will be using an active object, but the process would be the same for any other object placed on the screen.

1. Create a new TGF2 application by clicking on the New button, or using the File>New menu option.

2. Double left-click on text Frame 1 in the Workspace toolbar window to access the blank frame.

3. Right-click on the frame area and select Insert > Object from the popup menu.

4. Select the Active object by single left-clicking on it and then click on the OK button.

5. Your mouse cursor will change to a crosshair. Now left-click anywhere on the frame to place the object.

6. The active object will be placed on screen and automatically the Object Property window will display the object properties. Click on the Movement tab in the Properties window (this is the graphic of the running man).

7. You will now see the Movement Property window as shown in Figure 6.1.

Figure 6.1
The default Movement Property.

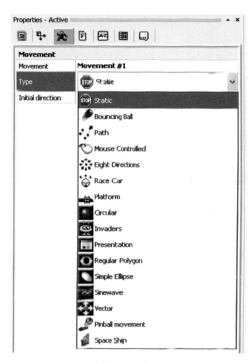

Figure 6.2
The movement types available in TGF2.

There are three basic options available, Movement, Type, and Initial Direction. Both Movement and Initial Direction can be clicked on, but when the object is set to static, these options will have no effect. We will discuss these options and how they work with movement shortly.

To access all of the available movement properties available in TGF2, you need to click on the Static button across from the Type property. You will then see the movement types available in TGF2, as shown in Figure 6.2.

Within the Type list are two types of movement objects. The first is configured through Properties and then any additional movement is applied to the object through the Event Editor. So in the case of the Active object, we would set actions via the Active Object icon in the editor.

The second type are special movements which require an additional object, called the Clickteam Movement Controller, to be placed onscreen, and any programming will be accessed via this object in the Event Editor. We will cover this later in this chapter.

First, we will need to take a look at the first group of Movement Type. These include:

▶ **Bouncing Ball**

▶ **Path**

▶ **Mouse Controlled**

▶ **Eight Directions**

▶ **Race Car**

▶ **Platform**

▶ **Pinball**

Bouncing Ball Movement

When you want an object to react like a bouncing ball, you can apply the Bouncing Ball Movement. The bouncing ball movement can also be configured in such a way as to create other types of movements; for example, a set of alien spaceships moving diagonally across the screen. It is important to remember that even though the default settings are set up in such a way as to create a specific movement type, you can also use it in other ways. This is more so the case with the bouncing ball movement than any of the other movement types.

Using the Active object that we added to the frame, ensure that the movement tab is selected and is set to Bouncing Ball as shown in Figure 6.3. You will then see the movement properties as shown in Figure 6.4.

Figure 6.3
The Bouncing Ball icon.

There are a number of important settings for the Bouncing Ball movement, inclduing:

▶ **Initial Direction:** This is the direction in which the object will move when the frame is first run. If you click on the initial direction list of numbers, you will be presented with a circle surrounded by a number of arrows and squares as shown in Figure 6.5. The icon on the bottom left will remove all directions, while the icon on the right will add all directions.

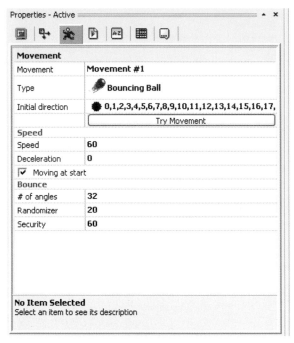

Figure 6.4
The Bouncing Ball properties.

▶ **Speed:** You can set the speed of the object. The default is 60, but you can increase it if you want it to move faster and decrease it to make it go slower.

▶ **Ball Deceleration:** If the ball hits a wall or another object, you can make it slow down. The default setting is 0, which means that it will continue to bounce forever.

▶ **Moving at Start:** Do you want the object to be moving as soon as the frame starts? If so, leave the checkbox checked. This is the default option, but if you uncheck it, you will need to start the movement for the object in the Event Editor.

▶ **# of Angles:** By default, there are 32 directions (angles) that the ball can move in. If you don't want to use this many, you can reduce the number of angles using the drop-down box. You can set this number to 16 or 8 instead of 32.

▶ **Bounce Randomizer:** If you want the ball to bounce in a predictable direction, for example, based on the angle of it hitting an object, you would ensure the number is lower for bounce randomization. If you want a more varied bounce, where it could go in a totally different direction than expected, increase this number.

▶ **Bounce Security:** When the ball bounces, there is always a chance that it could bounce a number of times in the same direction. For example, it could bounce up and down in the same direction multiple times. If you are creating a bat and ball game, you will not want it to do this, so you would increase this number.

Initial Starting Directions

If you place multiple starting directions, TGF2 will randomly select a direction from those that are enabled.

Adding and Removing Directions

You can add or remove a specific direction by clicking on the black box in the Direction dialog box.

Direction Numbers

In TGF2, there are a maximum of 32 movement directions. Each direction is given a number from 0 to 31. You can tell TGF2 to move an object in a particular direction by telling it the direction number in the Event Editor.

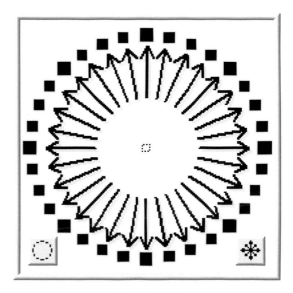

Figure 6.5
The directions available to select and deselect.

There are two ways of testing your newly configured movement. You can click on the Try Movement button in the Movement properties (Object Properties window). This will show you the object bouncing around the screen, and you can then decide if you need to make any changes to the relevant properties.

The second option is to run the frame or application using the F7 or F8 keys or clicking the buttons on the Button toolbar.

The big difference with these two options is that when you use the Try Movement button, it creates a window that will make the object bounce around the screen. This is to show you what the movement will be like with the configuration changes you have made. When you actually run your game, the ball will fly off in a direction, get to the edge of the screen, and then fly off the screen. This is because in reality although you have given the ball movement you haven't configured any logic to your game to prevent the ball going off the screen. This is because you may actually want it to go off a specific part of the screen, so TGF2 doesn't have this configured by default.

To stop the ball from bouncing around the screen, you will need to go into the Event Editor and program it:

1. Click on the Event Editor button to enter the Event Editor. You will see a blank Event Editor with one event line with the words New Condition on it.

2. Click on New Condition to create your event line. We want to test the position of the ball (in this case, a green diamond). So the condition will be against the active object, so in the dialog box right-click on the green active object and select Position > Test Position of Active as shown in Figure 6.6.

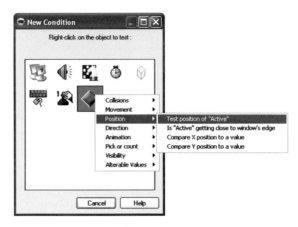

Figure 6.6
The test object Position location on the popup menu.

3. A new dialog box will appear. This is the Test position of "Active" dialog box, and it allows you to quickly click on areas of the screen that you wish to check for. We want the four arrows pointing outwards as shown in Figure 6.7. Click on OK to save the direction to the Event Editor.

4. You will now have a single condition on the event line, which reads active (graphic) Leaves the play area.

Test Position Options

In Figure 6.7, there are several tests you can do for object placement. The first four arrows you previously selected were checking to see if an object was about to leave the screen, from the left, right, top, or bottom of the screen. The four arrows pointing inward will check to determine whether any object is about to enter the frame. The big arrow in the middle of the dialog box is a general test to see if the object is in the frame, regardless of its position. Finally, the large arrow on the bottom left corner is checking to see if the object is on the outside of the frame, again regardless of its general position.

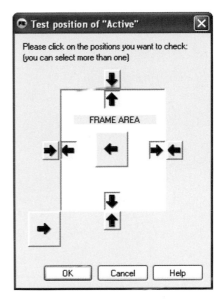

Figure 6.7
The Test Position of "Active" dialog box with four outward positions tested.

5. We now want the ball to bounce when it hits any of these edges, so we need to add an action. Move to the right of this event until you are directly under the active object and right-click on the blank action box. Select the Movement > Bounce option. You will now see your event and action as shown in Figure 6.8.

On running the program, by pressing F7 or F8, you will see the ball moving around the screen, and when it hits the edge of the application window, it will bounce back. In your own games, you might want to not stop the ball going off the screen in a specific direction. To do this, you would just not select the arrow that corresponds to that side of the screen.

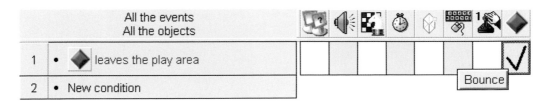

Figure 6.8
The final event and action for the bouncing ball to move around the screen.

Path Movement

Path movement allows you to tell an object where to move on the screen using a number of points, called *nodes*. You are able to draw the path of where you want the object to move and configure such things as its speed and whether or not it should reverse its movement. Using the same active object we configured for bouncing ball movement, you can access its properties and change the Type drop-down to Path. You can see the Path icon and the properties it displays once it's selected in Figures 6.9 and 6.10.

Figure 6.9
The Path movement icon.

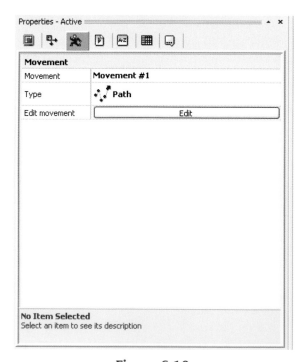

Figure 6.10
The Properties window for the path movement.

As you can see in Figure 6.10, there are no properties available for this movement within the Properties window. To create a path for the active object, you need to click on the Edit button. This will open an external editor as shown in Figure 6.11. We have also labeled the relevant buttons, but you can see what they are called by hovering the mouse cursor over the button. A text tooltip will appear.

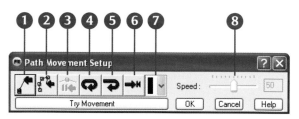

Figure 6.11
The Path Movement Setup dialog box.

1. **Newline:** Create a brand new path movement line. This will be created from the object to the mouse pointer cursor. You will then need to click on the frame to place at the end of the line, called a node.

2. **Tape Mouse:** This allows you to draw your path using the mouse, in the same way you can paint a line on a drawing package. Holding down the left mouse button as you move the cursor over the frame will draw the path.

3. **Set a Pause:** If you want your object to stop at a specific point (node), you can create a pause. First, you must select the node upon which you want to create the pause, and then click on the Pause button. An additional dialog box will appear as shown in Figure 6.12, where you type in the time for the pause.

4. **Loop the Movement:** This will make the movement follow the same path over and over again.

5. **Reverse at End:** When it gets to the last node, the object will return back along the same path. For example if you have two points, A and B, connected by a line, the object will move from point A to B, and if Reverse at End is selected, the object will then move back from point B to point A.

6. **Reposition Object at End:** This will return the object to its starting position.

7. **Node Color:** The default color of your path and its nodes is black, but if you are running a game with a black background, you will not be able to see the path. You are able to change the lines to something else.

8. **Speed:** You can change the speed between each node from the default of 50. The lower the number, the slower it will go; the higher, the faster.

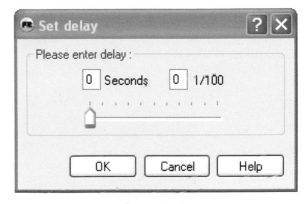

Figure 6.12
Use this dialog box to choose the time for the pause.

Moving Nodes

You can move the exact position of a node by holding down the left mouse button over a node square and then dragging it to a new position.

If you want to test the movement, you can click on the Try Movement button, and then watch it work. If you want to quit the test, you can press the Escape key in the top left corner of your keyboard or click the Stop button in the dialog box that appears. If you want to save the movement to the object, click on the OK button; otherwise, click on Cancel. You can see an example of a path movement in Figure 6.13.

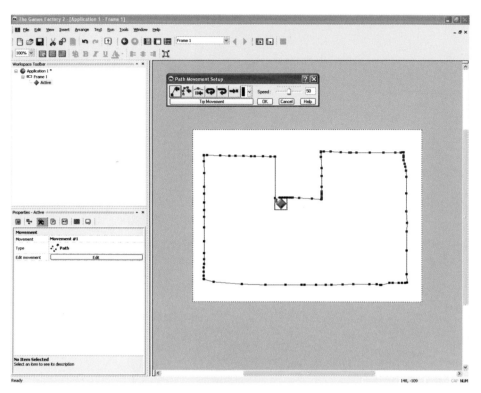

Figure 6.13
An example of a path created using the tape mouse option.

Looping Movement

If you use Loop Movement, you may find
that the object disappears off the screen.
This is because when you use just Loop
Movement, the object will begin the same
path from its current position onscreen. So if
you have a path that makes the object move
to the right, it will continue to move right
until it disappears off screen. If you don't
want it to disappear, you can use Reposition
Object at End to place it back at the very first
node position on the screen.

You can also access additional information and
properties by right-clicking on a node. You can
create another line, use tape mouse, set a pause
or its speed, and name a node. You can also
delete a line. The majority of these you will
access through the path editor dialog except for
Set Name. Setting a name is a useful option as
you can tell the object to go to a node using its
name through the Event Editor.

Mouse Controlled

When you want an object to be controlled by the mouse, you can select the Mouse Controlled option. The Mouse Controlled option makes any object follow the mouse cursor. It also makes the standard mouse cursor disappear. You can see the mouse controlled icon and the default properties in Figures 6.14 and 6.15.

Figure 6.14
The Mouse Controlled icon in the Type drop-down menu.

Figure 6.15
The properties of the Mouse Movement.

You can see in Figure 6.15 that the Mouse Controlled option has a Player field. This allows you to configure this type of movement to a specific player. There are no other options within the properties, and further configuration is required via the Edit button.

When you click the Edit button, a dotted line appears around the object, as shown in Figure 6.16, and a mouse movement dialog box appears. This dotted line represents the area where this object will be able to move around in the frame. At the moment this area isn't very big, and you can expand it by holding down the left mouse button on one of the black boxes and dragging the box to where you want it.

Once you are happy with the area in which the object will move, click on Try movement to test it, or click on OK to save the information. If you do run the application, you will need to use Alt + F4 to close it.

Limited Mouse Control

When making games, you must be careful that you include an option for the user to easily exit an application. In the previous example, we have set the mouse area, but this then removes the ability for the user (in this case, you) to be able to close the application by clicking on the red x in the top right corner. Whenever you use the mouse controlled option, you must allow for other ways of closing the application or exiting from that frame and returning to another screen. A good way to do that is to use the Esc (escape) key to exit.

Saving the Settings

Your settings won't be saved until you click on the OK button, and if you click on Cancel, the changes you made since the last edit will be lost.

Eight Directions

One of the most common ways of controlling a game character, spaceship, or object is to use the keyboard arrow keys. In fact, there are two sets of these keys on the keyboard. First there are the up, down, left, and right keys; then there are eight keys that are available on the number pad (usually the set of number keys on the right side of the keyboard). You can see an example of the number pad and arrow keys in Figure 6.17.

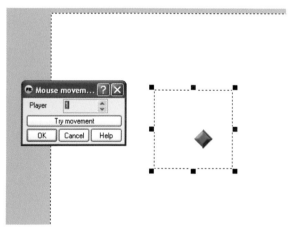

Figure 6.16
The Mouse Controlled dialog box and the mouse movement area.

Number Pad Keys

To use the keys on the number pad, you must ensure that the Num Lock key has been switched off. You can normally tell if it's switched off if there is no Num Lock light on the keyboard.

Moving the Object

If you move the object, the dotted box area will move with the object, so you may need to reposition the mouse area box if you move objects on the screen.

Figure 6.17
An example of the arrow and number pad keys.

The Eight Directions icon can be seen in Figure 6.18, and its properties are shown in Figure 6.19. As you can see from Figure 6.19, there are a number of options available in the dialog box.

 **Eight Directions**

Figure 6.18
The Eight Directions icon.

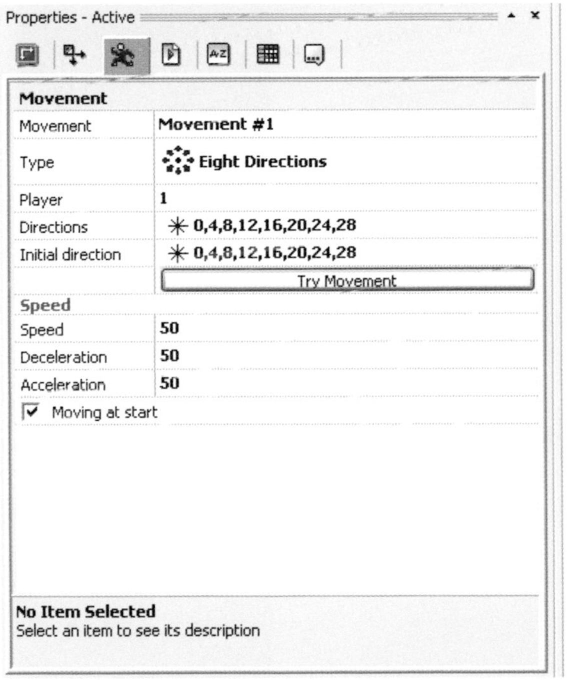

Figure 6.19
The Eight Directions Properties dialog box.

These properties are:

▶ **Player:** You can assign the eight directions movement to a particular player.

▶ **Directions:** Using the same direction dialog as the bouncing ball object, you can select the directions that the object can move in using the arrow and number pad keys.

▶ **Initial Direction:** This is the initial direction that the object can move in. Again using the standard direction dialog, you can select and deselect the directions by clicking on them using the mouse.

▶ **Speed:** This is the speed of the object. The default speed is 50; the lower the number, the slower it goes and the higher, the faster.

▶ **Deceleration:** When the player releases the keys, how quickly will the object slow down and then come to a stop? The default is 50. If you want the object to stop as soon as the key is released, change Deceleration to 0. Increasing this number increases the distance the object travels before stopping.

▶ **Acceleration:** This defines how long the object will take to reach its set maximum speed. If you want the object to take longer to get up to top speed, you can decrease this number.

You can easily test the movement of your object by pressing F7 and then using the arrow keys to move around the screen. You can also move in a diagonal direction if you hold down both the left and up, right and up, left and down, or right and down keys.

Race Car

If you want to create a racing car game or give an object the ability to react like a car, then Race Car movement is the option to select. You might think this seems a very similar movement to the eight direction movement, which is also a good choice for car movement. There are some subtle differences, however, that will make a difference to which of the two movements you pick for any racing games you make. The main difference is that the object can turn at an angle, and you can reverse and turn at the same time. So you can make the object look like a car moving and turning. The keys used for the movement of the car can be seen in Table 6.1.

Table 6.1 Keys Used for the Race Car Movement

Action	Keyboard
Accelerate	Up Arrow
Brake	Down Arrow
Reverse	Down Arrow
Turn Left	Left Arrow
Turn Right	Right Arrow

Figure 6.20
The Race Car icon.

You can see the Race Car icon and Properties window in Figures 6.20 and 6.21.

There are only two additional options that you haven't seen in any of the other movements. These are the Enable Reverse and the Rotating Speed options. By enabling reverse, you can press the down arrow key to stop the object and then press it again to make the object reverse backwards. The rotating speed defines how quickly the object will rotate when it is turning.

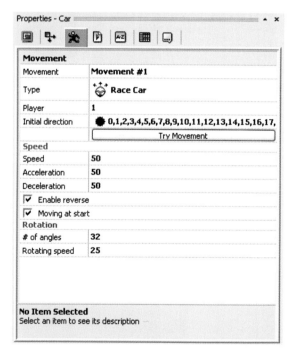

Figure 6.21
The Race Car Properties window.

Platform

If you are thinking about making a platform game where a character moves along a series of platforms, climbs up ladders, and jumps between floors, then you need to use the Platform movement. The Platform movement takes a little more work to get set up initially than all of the other movements as you need to take into account the platforms and ladder graphic configurations as well as configuring the player character.

Movement of the character or graphic that is given the Platform movement will, by default, be controlled by the arrow keys and the Shift key to jump.

To create a platform game, you will need to complete the following tasks:

1. Place a number of graphic backdrop objects onto your frame that will represent your ladders, platforms, and elevators.

2. Configure the properties of these backdrop objects by accessing their runtime tab and configuring the obstacle type.

3. Create your character as an active object, and change its movement to platform. Configure any other properties you require.

4. Create some event code to prevent the player character from falling through any platforms, which it will do by default.

You can see the icon for the Platform movement and its Properties window in Figures 6.22 and 6.23.

Figure 6.22
The Platform icon in the Type drop down box.

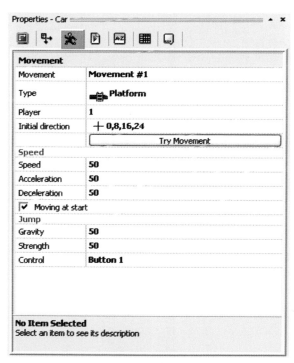

Figure 6.23
The Platform movement properties.

Some of the options that are important to this object are:

- ▶ **Gravity: This option affects the gravity of the object. A high setting makes your character fall more quickly, while a lower figure makes it slow down. This will also affect the height of a jump, and a lower figure will only allow for a shorter distance.**

- ▶ **Strength: This affects the jumping power of your character.**

- ▶ **Jump Controls: Here you can select from one of four options from a drop down box. Button 1 allows the fire button of a joystick or the Shift key to make the character jump. Button 2 means the second fire button on the joystick and the Ctrl key to activate a jump, while no jump means the character cannot jump, and finally up left/right arrow makes the left and right arrow keys activate the jump.**

To complete the process of creating a platform game, you need to do the event programming to prevent the character from falling off the screen. On the CD-ROM that accompanies this book, a simple example file has been created for you. Locate the example in the Movements folder and open the file called platform-movement.mfa. You will see a small creature, two rows of platform, and a single ladder as shown in Figure 6.24.

If you click on the platform and/or the ladder and check the Runtime tab of its properties, you will see the obstacle type is set to Platform and Ladder, as shown in Figures 6.25 and 6.26.

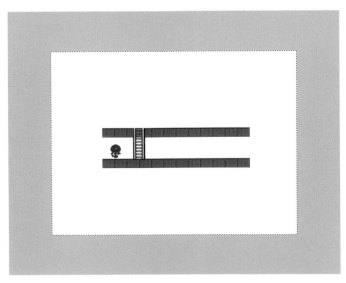

Figure 6.24
A simple example platform game.

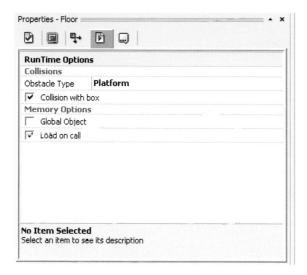

Figure 6.25
The Platform setting in Obstacle type.

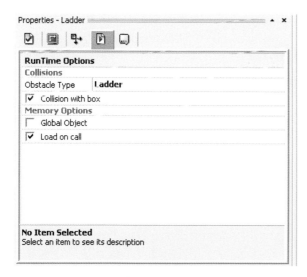

Figure 6.26
The Ladder setting in Obstacle type.

If you were to run this program now, nothing would happen because currently the player character is set to static. You will need to change the player character to have the platform movement.

1. Click on the fish-like creature called Blinky.

2. Click on the Movement tab of the object properties.

3. Change it from Static to Platform movement.

Press F7 to run the game and watch the Blinky character fall through the platform and off the screen. This now requires some game logic to be written in the Event Editor to stop the character from falling through the platform.

To do this, we need to do the following:

1. Click on the Event Editor button.

2. You will be presented with a blank Event Editor screen.

3. We will now program a condition that will check for a collision between our character Blinky and the backdrop object (remember, all of our platform objects are backdrops). Click on the New condition text.

4. Because we want to test against Blinky, right-click on the Blinky graphic to reveal the popup menu. Then select Collisions > Backdrop. You have now created the event and are ready to create the action.

5. The action we want is quite simple. We want to tell the object to stop moving. This action will only prevent it from moving downward and won't prevent the object from moving left or right. Move across until you are directly under the Blinky object, right-click on the action box, and select Movement > Stop.

6. Your event and action will look like Figure 6.27.

Pinball Movement

Remember, you will need to program the code in the Event Editor to prevent the ball from falling off the screen. This is done using the Test position option and then using the action Bounce.

Pinball

If you want to create a pinball game or any game where a ball will have gravity applied to it, you can use the Pinball movement. In many cases, you might use the Bouncing ball for standard ball movement, but that does not have any gravity options, so the Pinball option is very specific to games where you need this feature.

If you have played a pinball machine, you know that the ball can increase and decrease in speed, depending on its being hit by a paddle or encountering other obstacles. The most important aspect is that the ball is always trying to get to the bottom of the board. This is gravity having an effect on the ball, just as it does when you throw a ball into the air. When using the Bouncing ball movement, if the ball is thrown upward, it will continue to move in the same direction.

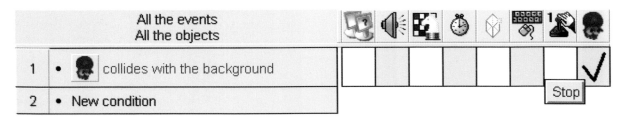

Figure 6.27
The event, condition, and action to prevent the Blinky character from falling through the platform.

You can see the Pinball icon and its Properties window in Figures 6.28 and 6.29.

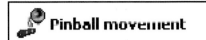

Figure 6.28
The Pinball movement icon.

Figure 6.29
The Pinball movement Properties.

Other Available Movements

There are another eight movement types included with TGF2 that were written by a third party. These add special movement features to TGF2 and allow you to really configure unique games with ease, where before you might have had to make your own special movement engine using code in the Event Editor.

The additional movement types that are available are:

▶ **Circular:** This can be used if you want to create circular-based movement, for example, spiral effects or objects rotating around other objects.

▶ **Invaders:** Space Invaders is a very popular type of old game, where you would have waves of enemy ships moving in tandem down the screen. This effect can be created by manually using code in the Event Editor; alternatively, using this movement will reduce the hassle of needing to create the code for moving set amounts of space and then changing directions.

▶ **Presentation:** If you have ever wanted to create a presentation or a game with text that scrolls on and off screen, this movement type will make it a breeze. You can select many different text entry and exit options from within the properties dialog box.

▶ **Regular Polygon:** A polygon is a shape that is connected by a number of straight lines. These straight lines will be in a closed format, which means all line ends connect to one another. A triangle, square, or rectangle can all be classed as polygons. Using polygon movement means that an object can move around these polygon shapes.

▶ **Simple Ellipse:** An ellipse is like a squashed circle. If you think of a shape that the bottom of a cone makes, this is usually an ellipse. This movement option allows you to make objects move in an elliptical shape.

▶ **Sinewave:** Sinewave allows you to move objects from one point to another while also moving them in a wave effect. If you think of a wave in the ocean, you can make an object move in this way from one point to another.

▶ **Vector:** The Vector movement is very powerful and allows for many different movement types, with acceleration and velocity vectors. Vector movement has many movement options available to it in the Event Editor.

▶ **Spaceship:** In some games you may want to create a spaceship. This spaceship might have a thruster, an engine that can move it in one direction and increase its velocity.

These movement types work in a slightly different way than the other ones we previously mentioned. You apply them in the same way by clicking on the object, accessing the object Properties Movement tab, and clicking on the Type drop down box. In the first set of objects we talked about, you would configure any actions on the object that you want to do the action with. For example, when you want an object to bounce, you would access these properties against the active object you set the Bouncing ball movement on.

These additional movement types have additional properties and configuration options but are accessed through a separate object that you need to add to the frame before you can access these additional functions. We will go through this process to show you how it works for these objects:

1. Create your game file and create your frames.

2. Add any objects.

3. Configure any movements.

4. You would now be ready to add the additional movement controller, right-click on the frame. and select Insert > Object.

5. Select the object Clickteam Movement Controller. You can see the Objects icon in Figure 6.30.

Clickteam
Moveme...

Figure 6.30
The icon for the Clickteam Movement Controller.

6. The object itself does not have any important options in its properties. Click on the Event Editor button to access the Event Editor.

7. To see the object in action, you need to create a single event line so you can view the object Properties. Click on New Condition text and select the Storyboard Controls icon; then right-click and select Start of Frame.

8. Move across to the Clickteam Movement Controller and right-click. You will now see several menus as shown in Figure 6.31. These are the options for the other movement options available.

Movement Controller

You will not be able to access any of the special movement options for an object until you have added the Movement Controller. Both the type of movement and the extra movement options in the action box are reliant on each other, so even if the Movement Controller has been added, you will not be able to use the movement options until you have selected a corresponding movement in the Type drop down box.

Multiple Movements

You have learned all about the different movement types available in TGF2, but you may have noticed one option in the Movement tab that we haven't discussed. There is an option that is displayed as Movement #1. This is the default movement number, and by clicking on it, you can create many different movements for a single object. This means that for a single object you could create movement #1 as a Bouncing ball, movement #2 as Path, and movement #3 as Pinball. This allows you a large amount of power to configure individual objects with different movements and then switch them on and off when needed.

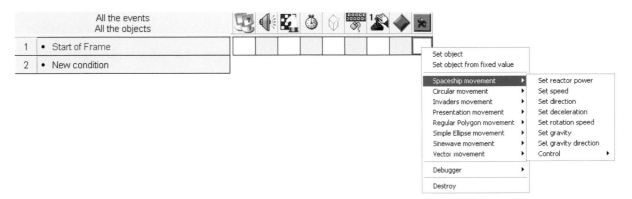

Figure 6.31
Some of the options available through the Event Editor for the Clickteam Movement Controller.

This is particularly useful for computer-controlled enemies, because you could create a path movement for them to move around a set path on the screen. Once they get within a set distance from the player, you could then change the movement to Bouncing ball and make them move towards the character.

To access additional movements:

1. Ensure that you have an active object added to the frame. Click on the object to access its movement.

2. Click on the text Movement #1. This will bring up a + and − sign. Click on it.

3. A Movements dialog box will appear as shown in Figure 6.32. You will see a single default movement that was added to the object when it was created.

4. By clicking on the Create New button, you can create additional movements.

Changing Movements

To change among different movements you have set up, you must use the Event Editor.

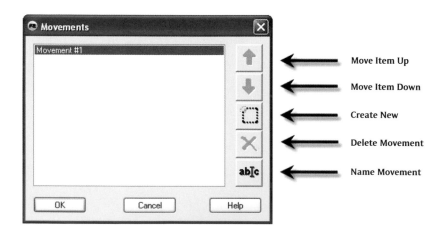

Figure 6.32
The dialog box for adding multiple movements.

start

Pictures and
Animations

CREATING GAMES WITH BUILT-IN GRAPHICS is a quick way of getting a game up and running quickly. In many cases, you may want to import or draw your own. This is possible with the built-in Picture and Animation Editor.

If you are a talented artist but could never program, then TGF2 is the perfect platform for you to use to make games. If you aren't that good at making your own graphics, then you have the option of importing images you have scanned, or photos taken with a digital camera. Either way, you most likely will spend some time in the Picture Editor.

In this chapter, we will look at the interface to the Picture and Animation Editor and show how to import images and use the built-in tools to draw your own. We will also look at how to animate your own characters to create interesting and fun animations.

The Picture Editor

THE PICTURE EDITOR CAN be accessed in several different ways, but the most common is by double-clicking on an active object in the Frame Editor. You may also find yourself accessing it by clicking on an edit button in the object or application properties.

To access the Picture Editor using an active object, you can:

► **Create a new TGF2 application by clicking on the New button or using the Ctrl and N key combination.**

► **Double-click on the text Frame 1 in the Workspace toolbar.**

► **Right-click on the frame and select Insert > Object. From the object list, select the Active object.**

► **Click on the frame to place the object. Double-click on the green diamond object. This will display the Picture and Animation Editor as shown in Figure 7.1.**

Note

Although the actual name is Picture and Animation Editor, in general use, that is shortened to Picture Editor in TFG2.

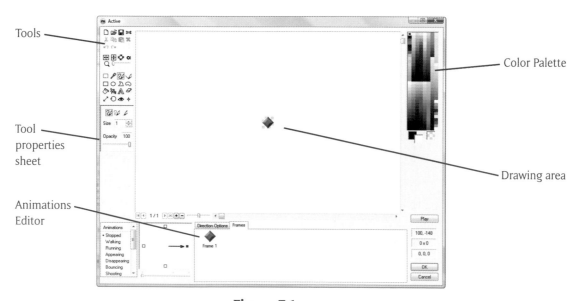

Figure 7.1
The Picture Editor displayed after double-clicking on an active object.

In Figure 7.1 you can see the following areas on the Picture Editor:

1. Tools

2. Tool properties sheet

3. Drawing area

4. Color Palette

5. Animations Editor

Tools

The drawing tools shown in Figure 7.2 are a standard set of features that you would find in graphic creation programs. If you have used Adobe Photoshop, Fireworks, Microsoft Paint, or any other paint package, you may recognize some of these tools already.

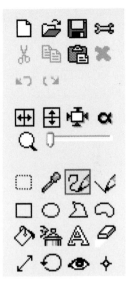

Figure 7.2
The drawing tools for the Picture Editor.

Tooltips

If you hold the mouse cursor over the tool icon, you will be presented with a popup box containing the name of that tool.

Figure 7.3
The Clear image option.

Clear

This option, shown in Figure 7.3, will clear/remove any image that is currently in the drawing area. This is something you will use a lot because you will always want to replace the active object's green diamond with a different graphic. You may also use it to delete a graphic you're working on if you aren't happy with it.

Clear Shortcut

You can also use the shortcut keys of Ctrl+N to clear the picture.

Undo

If you clear the image and decide you want to put it back, you can press Ctrl+Z to undo the clear.

Figure 7.4
The Import option icon.

Import

It is very likely that at some point you will want to import an image from your computer. Perhaps it's an image you drew yourself in another paint package or an image from a digital camera. The Import option, shown in Figure 7.4, also works with multiple images, which allow you to import animations in one quick and easy process.

▶ **PNG: Portable Network Graphics format. This is a very popular web and printing file format, which allows lossless data compression. The file size of the image is made smaller without the loss of overall quality of the image.**

▶ **JPEG: Joint Photographic Experts Group. This format has been one of the most popular for displaying images on a web page. Using compression, it can reduce the file size of the image, thus making the file smaller than PNG files, but not without an effect on the overall quality of the image.**

▶ **GIF: Graphics Interchange Format. This is another format that was widely used on the Internet, again because it could reduce the file size of an image. Over the last few years, it has become less popular due to licensing issues, so it has generally been replaced by PNG.**

▶ **FLC: Originally used in a program called Autodesk, this is a simple animation format that plays a set of images quickly to create an animation.**

▶ **BMP: Also known as Bitmap, this file type is a very common format in paint packages. Files are generally larger than in many other formats.**

▶ **PCX: This very early file format was used in some early graphics packages. Generally considered obsolete, but it is available if required.**

Graphics Formats for Games

The best formats to use for your games are BMP and PNG. PNG is the best format to use overall because it will also make the file format smaller. Both formats keep the standard of the graphics at a high quality. If you are creating a simple game for the Internet, then you might want to consider looking at JPG and reducing the quality to a level that is acceptable for your game.

Import Quick Key

You can quickly open the Import dialog box by using the Ctrl+O keys.

Export

The Export option shown in Figure 7.5 allows you to export any images you have in TGF2 and save them as BMP, PNG, or JPG formatted files. If you have an animation (multiple images), you can save them out to a set of image files.

The importance of the Export option becomes more apparent when you have either drawn your own images in the Picture Editor or amended pre-loaded images, and you want to store them on your machine for use in other games.

Figure 7.5
The Export option icon.

Export Quick Key

You can launch the Export dialog box by pressing the Ctrl+S key combination.

Options

The Options button allows you to configure the Picture Editor preferences; you can see the Options icon in Figure 7.6. When drawing on the canvas you can set-up a background color or colors, this helps with seeing where there is currently no pixels (where it is transparent). By default these colors are grey and white and are the most common background in paint packages.

You can see the Picture Editor Preferences dialog box in Figure 7.7. You are able to configure how the right mouse button will react in the Picture Editor, whether it will draw a pixel color or get the current color at the mouse pointer location.

Figure 7.6
The Options icon.

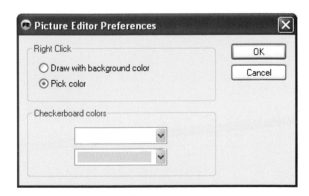

Figure 7.7
The Picture Editor Preferences dialog box.

Cut, Copy, Paste, and Delete

When you are drawing images on the canvas, you may find that you want to delete what you've done, paste content from another image, cut out part of an image, or copy a section of the image. You can do all of this using the Cut, Copy, Paste, and Delete buttons as shown in Figure 7.8.

Figure 7.8
The Cut, Copy, Paste, and Delete buttons.

The buttons do the following:

▶ **Cut: The area on the image is cut out and replaced by the transparent checkerboard color. You will have to use the selection tool to highlight the area on the image.**

▶ **Copy: The area that is highlighted on the image using the selection tool is copied on to the Windows clipboard. The original image is left intact.**

▶ **Paste: Any image that is currently stored in the Windows clipboard will be pasted into the current image on the canvas.**

▶ **Delete: Any area on the canvas that has been selected is immediately deleted.**

The Selection Tool

We will cover the selection tool shortly.

Undo and Redo

If you want to either undo a set of pixels you have drawn on the canvas or reapply a change you have undone, you can use the Undo and Redo buttons as shown in Figure 7.9.

Figure 7.9
The Undo and Redo buttons.

Redo and Undo

As with many other programs, if you make a mistake and you want to undo it, you can use Ctrl+Z, and if you want to reapply the change you have undone, you can use Ctrl+Y.

Flip Horizontally

This tool, shown in Figure 7.10, will take the image that is currently displayed on the canvas and flip it over. This will swap your image from left to right, so it would be the same as looking in a mirror; the image that you can see is the new image.

Flip Vertically

This tool, shown in Figure 7.10, will flip the image from top to bottom, which will turn the image upside down.

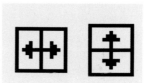

Figure 7.10
The Flip horizontally and Flip vertically icons.

Flipping the Graphic

If you flip the graphic and decide that you do not want it displayed in this new position, you can either use the Undo button or you can click the same flip button a second time to set it back to its original position.

Flipping the Image Quick Keys

You can flip the image vertically by using the Ctrl+J keys, and horizontally by using the Ctrl+I keys.

Crop

When you draw an image on a canvas or import an image onto a canvas which is larger than the image, you might have a large white space. This transparent space is where there are currently no pixels and is effectively wasted space. You can crop an image, which will remove this blank space from around an image. The crop icon can be seen in Figure 7.11.

Figure 7.12
The Transparency icon.

Figure 7.11
The Crop image icon.

Crop Quick Key

You can crop the image automatically by using the Ctrl+ K keys.

Figure 7.13
The Transparency Properties box.

Transparency

Transparency is a section of an image that is clear, and you will be able to see straight through it to any images behind it. You can display and hide the current transparency color by clicking the icon in Figure 7.12; you will also get an option to switch it on or off in the Tools Properties window as shown in Figure 7.13.

Transparency Quick Key

You can change to the Transparency tool by pressing the Y key.

Zoom

When you are drawing an image, you might want to have more precision drawing of pixels on to the canvas. To do this, you need to zoom in as close as possible so you can have pixel perfect positioning; you can do this using the Zoom bar as shown in Figure 7.14.

To zoom, you need to hold down the left mouse button and drag to the left or to the right. Moving to the right zooms inward, and dragging the bar to the left will zoom out.

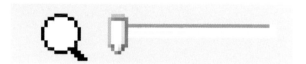

Figure 7.14
The Zoom bar.

Zooming Using the Mouse

You can also zoom in and out if you have a middle mouse button on your mouse. Rolling the button toward you zooms in, and pushing the middle mouse button away from you zooms outward.

The Selection Tool

Using the Selection tool, you can select a rectangular block, which you can then cut or copy from the image. This tool is used in conjunction with the Cut, Copy, Paste, and Delete buttons we discussed earlier. First, you would select the area that you wish to make changes to, and then use the other buttons to make the relevant change. You can see the Selection tool in Figure 7.15.

Figure 7.15
The Selection tool icon.

Selection Tool

You will notice that the Selection tool only allows you to select a square or rectangular area. If you need to remove part of an image more precisely, you may find it easier to use a more advanced graphics program and then import the image back into TGF2.

Selection Tool Quick Key

You can change to the Selection tool by pressing the B key.

Color Picker

When you are drawing an image, sometimes you may want to get the exact color that is being used in another part of the image. When drawing with many different shades of similar colors, this might be a little difficult to do using the naked eye. The color picker icon shown in Figure 7.16 can be used to copy the color of a pixel at a specific location on the canvas.

To use the color picker, select the icon, then click on the canvas at the pixel location that you want to copy the color.

Figure 7.16
The Color Picker icon.

Color Picker Quick Key

You can change to the Color Picker tool by pressing the P key.

The Brush Tool

When you want to draw on the canvas, you can select the Brush tool. This will allow you to draw freehand by holding down the left mouse button and then pointing at the canvas to create your shape. You can see the icon that represents the Brush tool in Figure 7.17.

Figure 7.17
The Brush tool icon.

Brush Tool Quick Key

You can change to the Brush tool by pressing the D key.

The Line Tool

If you want to draw a straight line or several straight lines, you would find this difficult with the Brush tool, so the Line tool makes this easier, as shown in Figure 7.18. You can also select the thickness of the line by increasing the size option in the Toolbar properties box. The larger the number, the thicker the line will become.

Figure 7.18
The Line tool icon.

Line Quick Key

You can change to the Line tool by pressing the L key.

The Rectangle Tool

If you want to draw a rectangle or square shape quickly and easily, then you can use this tool. You can also choose to fill the shape that is created with another color. You can see the Rectangle tool icon and its properties in Figures 7.19 and 7.20.

By default, the Rectangle tool creates an unfilled (clear) rectangle; by selecting one of the other icons in the Tools options box, you can choose to fill it instead, with or without a border.

Figure 7.19
The Rectangle tool icon.

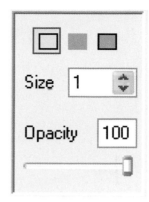

Figure 7.20
The Rectangle tool properties box.

Rectangle Quick Key

You can change to the Rectangle tool by pressing the R key.

The Ellipse Tool

An ellipse is a circle shape, and with the Ellipse tool you can draw a variety of circle-based images. When you click on the Ellipse tool, you hold down the left mouse button and then drag the cursor to create your circle-based shape. You can see the Ellipse icon and its property sheet in Figures 7.21 and 7.22.

Figure 7.21
The Ellipse icon.

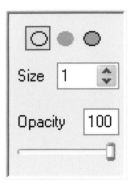

Figure 7.22
The Ellipse tools property box.

Drawing a Polygon

If you have drawn two lines, for example, and want the third line to join back to the starting line, just double-click to draw the final line automatically.

Ellipse Quick Key

You can change to the Ellipse tool by pressing the E key.

Figure 7.23
The Polygon button icon.

The Polygon Tool

A polygon is any shape that is created with straight lines that form a connecting shape. A triangle, square, and rectangle can all be considered polygons. The Polygon tool is very similar to the Line tool, where you draw a straight line, except once you have drawn a single line, it will then expect you to draw another line. It will only stop drawing lines when you have connected back to the original starting line. You can see the Polygon tool icon in Figure 7.23 and its properties in Figure 7.24.

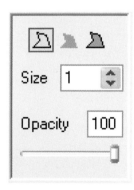

Figure 7.24
The Polygon tool property box.

Polygon Quick Key

You can change to the Polygon tool by pressing the G key.

The Shape Tool

The Shape tool lets you draw a non-uniform shape (without using straight lines) and when you take your finger off the left mouse button, it will close the shape automatically. The main difference between this and the Polygon tool is that this does not draw straight lines. You can see the icon for this tool in Figure 7.25 and its property box in Figure 7.26.

The Fill Tool

When you want to change the color in an enclosed space, you can use the Fill tool to change the area on the canvas to a single color. You can see the Fill icon and tool sheet in Figures 7.27 and 7.28.

Figure 7.27
The Fill tool icon.

Figure 7.25
The Shape tool icon.

Figure 7.28
The Fill tool property sheet.

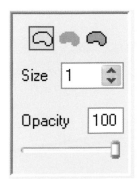

Figure 7.26
The Shape tool property box.

Fill Tool Leakage

If you have a gap in any area you intend to fill, the color that you use will also fill any other areas around it. This may cause graphical issues with your image, so it is always sensible to make sure you have no gaps in the image before using the Fill option.

Figure 7.29
The Spray tool icon.

Fill Tool Quick Key

You can change to the Fill tool by pressing the F key.

Figure 7.30
The Spray tool property box.

The Spray Tool

If you think about a spray can of paint, the Spray tool works in the same way. The longer you keep the spray can over a particular part of the canvas, the more pixels are covered in the selected color. You can change the size of the paint pixel and the amount of pressure that is applied. You can see the icon for the Spray tool in Figure 7.29 and its property box in Figure 7.30.

Spray Quick Key

You can change to the Spray tool by pressing the S key.

The Text Tool

Using the Text tool allows you to type a piece of text and then place it on the canvas. You can also apply standard text formatting to the text including bold, italic, and underline. You are also able to change the font type, so you can have text, which is more appropriate for your game. You can see the Text tool icon in Figure 7.31 and Its property sheet in Figure 7.32.

Figure 7.31
The Text tool icon.

Figure 7.32
The Text tool property sheet.

Text to Image

Once you have finished applying the text to the canvas, it is no longer a piece of text but is converted to an image, so you cannot re-edit the text.

Text Quick Key

You can change to the Text tool by pressing the T key.

Eraser Tool

If you want to delete part of your image, you can use the Eraser tool. This will allow you to rub out part of the image. You can increase the size of the eraser if you want to delete a larger area of the canvas; alternatively, you can make it smaller to make it more precise. The Eraser icon can be seen in Figure 7.33.

Figure 7.33
The Eraser tool icon.

Eraser Tool

If you want to delete large amounts of the canvas, you may want to do this in another graphics package and import it back into TGF2. The paint package in TGF2 is adequate for most jobs, but sometimes it is quicker to use a program that has been made solely to do graphics creation.

Eraser Quick Key

You can change to the Eraser by pressing the U key.

Size Tool

If you want to amend the size of your canvas, you can use the Resize option. You will also be given options to stretch the image, resample it, and make it proportional to the canvas size. You can see the icon for the Size tool in Figure 7.34 and its options in Figure 7.35.

Figure 7.34
The Size tool icon.

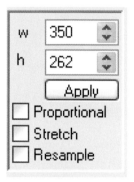

Figure 7.35
The Size tool property box.

Proportional, Stretch, Resample

The Proportional option will reduce both the width and height of the graphic the same number of pixels. This is useful when you want to amend the width and height by the same amount.

Using Stretch will amend the current image and stretch it to fit the new canvas size.

Using Resample will take the original image and resize it as best it can to the new canvas size, giving an overall better resizing quality.

Size Quick Key

You can change to the Size tool by pressing the W key.

Rotate

You may wish to rotate an image by a specific angle. Once you have selected the Rotate icon, shown in Figure 7.36, you will see the additional options in the Tools property sheet box in Figure 7.37. You can type in a number and then click Apply, or if you want to rotate by 90 degrees left or right, you can click on the additional buttons.

Figure 7.36
The Rotate icon.

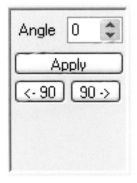

Figure 7.37
The Rotate properties sheet.

Rotation and Animations

Rotation of a graphic is very useful if you are creating animations. In an animation, you have multiple images, so you can make small direction changes to each image to create a rotation animation.

Rotate Quick Key

You can change to the Rotate tool by pressing the A key.

View Hot Spot

Every active object within TGF2 has a hot spot. This is an invisible marker that is attached to the graphic and is important when referencing its coordinates. For example, if you place the hot spot of a graphic to the bottom left of the image, and then tell TGF2 to place the object on the frame at the X coordinate of 0 and the Y coordinate of 0, the image will appear off frame. This is because the bottom left will be placed at zero while the rest of the image (above the hot spot) will be placed above this location. You can see the View Hot Spot icon in Figure 7.38.

In addition to manually setting the hot spot by using the left mouse button and clicking on the location on the image, you can also use the Quick Position button in the Tools property box. This provides you with a grid of nine boxes. Select one to quickly position the hot spot. You can see this in Figure 7.39.

Figure 7.38
The View Hot Spot icon.

Figure 7.39
The Hot Spot property box.

Frame Area

When viewing the visible frame area, the X and Y coordinate of 0,0 will be at the top left quadrant of the screen.

Hot Spot Quick Key

You can quickly check the hot spot by pressing the H key.

View Action Point

Within your games, you may want another graphic to appear from a specific part of the character; for example, you might want to show a bullet being fired from the character's weapon. To do this, you need to set an action point. By default, all active objects have a default action point in their top left corner. You can see the Action Point icon in Figure 7.40.

You can place the action point either by clicking on the image or by using the View Action property sheet. This property sheet looks the same as the Hot Spot property sheet in Figure 7.39. You can type in precise coordinates or use the Quick Move buttons.

Figure 7.40
The Action Point icon.

Action Point Quick Key

You can access the Action Point options by using the quick key of Q.

Drawing Area

There's not much to say about the drawing area. This is the area where you will see any imported images or draw on the canvas to create your picture. If you create an image that is too big for the canvas, the horizontal and vertical scrollbars will become enabled, which will allow you to scroll around the image.

You can see an image on the canvas in Figure 7.41.

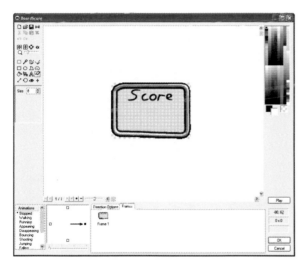

Figure 7.41
An image on the picture canvas.

The Color Palette

The Color Palette is a selection of color blocks, which you can select using the mouse buttons, that will then be used to color the canvas area. Below the Color Palette are three color boxes, two overlapping each other and one separate. The two boxes on the left are the current draw colors, which respond to the left and right mouse buttons on the canvas. The right box is the current transparency color.

You can see a close-up image of the Color Palette in Figure 7.42.

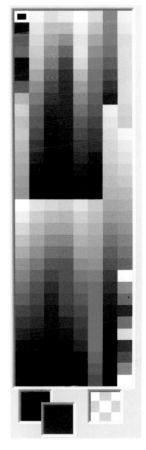

Figure 7.42
A close-up of the Color Palette.

The Animation Editor

WITHIN THE PICTURE EDITOR is the Animation Editor. This is located at the bottom of the Picture Editor, and when you create a new active object, you will by default see a single graphic in the Frames section.

An animation is a set of images played one after another, which then makes the graphic object look like it is animated. This could be a character waving its hand, a knight waving his sword, or a spaceship tilting to the left and right.

In most cases, the process for getting ready to create your animations would be that you have already drawn them in another art package or will make changes to images that you already have to create the animation. Normally, you would create a new active object on your frame, double-click on it, and then either draw or import a set of images.

The Animation Editor can be split into a number of parts, as shown in Figure 7.43.

These parts are as follows:

▶ **The Animation List: This is a list of all the different animations an object can have. The default starting animation is stopped, which means it will run when the object is not moving. We will discuss this in more detail shortly.**

▶ **The Directions: A graphic object can have as many as 32 directions. This is because if you were creating a game with a character, which could move upwards, to the left and right, and so on, you would need to create a set of animations for each direction that the character is facing.**

▶ **The Animation Frame Toolbar: These small icons show which frame you are currently on (1 of 1), and you can press the + or − buttons to add or remove frames. The slider allows you to scroll back and forth through all your animations.**

Figure 7.43
The Animation Editor in the Picture Editor.

▶ **Frames: This is a two-tabbed window, the Frames, which displays all of the individual images for the animation, and a second tab called Direction Options.**

▶ **Play Button: If you want to test what an animation looks like, clicking the Play button will launch a window which will then play all of the frames.**

To give you an idea of what a fully completed animation looks like, there is a completed animation of a flying dragon available on the CD-ROM that comes with this book.

1. Click on the File | Open option in TGF2.

2. When the browse box appears, navigate to the CD-ROM drive that contains the CD from the book. Navigate to the \Animation folder and select the dragonanimation.mfa file.

3. Once the file is loaded, double-click on the text Frame 1 in the Workspace toolbar to display the frame.

4. You will now see a dragon displayed on the desktop as shown in Figure 7.44.

5. Click the Run Application button or press F8 to launch the application. You will now see a flying dragon, animated as it moves its wings. Click on the red X in the top right corner of that application window to close the application.

6. We will now move to the Picture Editor and double-click on the dragon to access the Picture Editor.

7. You will now see the dragon on the canvas and a large number of frames, which are used to animate the dragon as it moves its wings as shown in Figure 7.45.

Figure 7.44
The dragon animated on a test application.

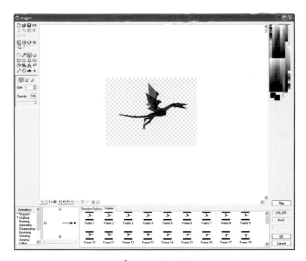

Figure 7.45
The animation frames of the dragon.

Clicking on the Dragon

You must ensure, when clicking on the dragon, that you click on the part of the image that contains colored pixels. Although the box surrounding the image is quite large, if you click on the transparent part (the bit that's white), TGF2 will launch an Insert an Object dialog box.

Leave the animation of the dragon loaded because we will use it as an example of how an animation is used in the Animation Editor.

The Animation List

The Animation List contains a set of 12 animations already pre-defined within TGF2. Each animation name can have as many as 32 directions assigned to it and many animation frames.

These animations are pre-programmed for certain aspects of your game, and in order to utilize them, all you need to do is draw or create your animations within them.

In Figure 7.46 for our loaded dragon animation, you can see that the first two animation names have a dot next to them. This means that they contain animation frames. For this animation of a dragon, the dots are beside the Stopped and Walking animations.

When using movement within TGF2, if your dragon is moving left or right, it will automatically play the Walking animation. It will then check to see if there is a set of animations for the direction the dragon is moving in, and if so, it will play them. In the case of Figure 7.47, you can see that there are animations for left and right because there are black squares in the Direction box.

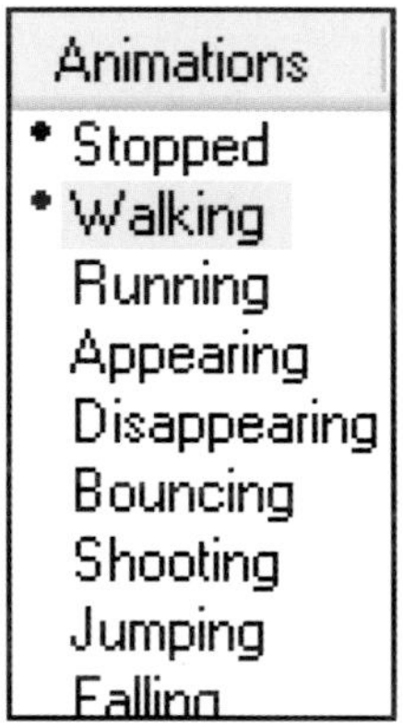

Figure 7.46
The Walking animation selected for our dragon example.

Animation Names

Additional animation names/groups can be added to the Animation list by right-clicking on the Animations box and selecting New. You can then name your animation and access it through the Event Editor.

Animations and Directions

Each direction will display the animation frames within the Frames box, but you cannot see all of them at one time. We will cover directions shortly.

Each animation set will run automatically when certain criteria have been met when the game is running. In the following list, you can see when this will happen:

▶ **Stopped:** When the graphic object is not moving (i.e., it is static).

▶ **Walking:** If the object is moving at a set speed (set in the Direction options tab against lower speed), it will play the animation that applies to walking.

▶ **Running:** If the object is moving at a set speed (against the higher speed in the Direction options tab), it will play the animation that applies to running.

▶ **Appearing:** The animation will start as soon as the object is created.

▶ **Disappearing:** Any animations will begin as the object is destroyed.

▶ **Bouncing:** When an object is bouncing onto another object (using the bouncing ball movement), it will play this animation set.

▶ **Shooting:** The animation starts when a shoot object action is created.

▶ **Jumping:** If platform movement is being used and a player graphic is told to jump, then this animation set will run.

▶ **Falling:** When an object is considered to be falling, the animation will play. The falling state is triggered when a player's character is set to Platform movement and it falls from a platform.

▶ **Climbing:** When using the platform movement, TGF2 will check for when the player is moving up a ladder and then play the Climbing animation.

▶ **Crouch Down:** This is another animation for the platform movement. You can make the character crouch down.

▶ **Stand Up:** When the character is not crouching down in the platform movement, it is considered to be standing up.

Directions and Direction Tab

When you click on any of the animations names listed in the Animation list, you will notice that each has a separate set of frames but also that they have a different set of directions. An example of this can be seen in Figure 7.47. In the left image, you can see that the Walking animation group is selected and the left direction tab is chosen. In the right image is the Walking animation group, but this time the right direction tab is chosen.

Default Number of Directions

The default number of directions for each animation set is always set to 4. You can increase this by using the slider under the directions box. You can increase it to a maximum of 32.

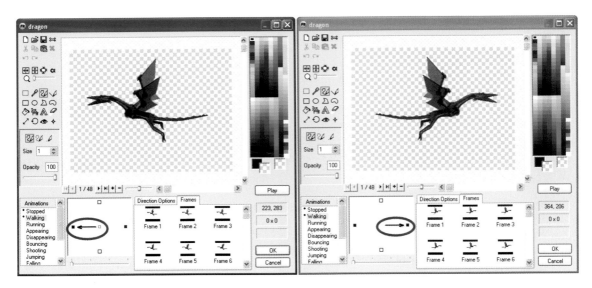

Figure 7.47
The Direction tab in use.

Creating Different Directions

You might think that creating animations for all of these different animation directions would be very time-consuming. You could either prepare the graphics in an external paint package before importing them, or alternatively, you could copy and paste the different frames. Once you have pasted the frames into the opposite direction, you can use the Flip and Rotate tools to get them pointing in the correct direction.

Direction Tab

If you click on the Direction tab, you will see a set of basic information about that particular direction. You can see in Figure 7.48 some information relating to the Dragon Animation, for the Walking group, and Right direction.

Within the Direction options tab, you will notice the Lower Speed and Higher speed buttons, where you can enter a number. The smallest number you can enter is 0 and the largest is 100. This speed is the speed of the animation and not the speed of the movement on the frame.

Creating a Bat and
Ball Game

I N CHAPTER 2, WE COVERED HOW to collate your ideas into potential game stories, creating the storyboards and thinking about the mechanics of a particular game. We covered a game called ChocoBreak, which is a bat and ball game. Now that you have covered many aspects of TGF2, it's time to create this game.

In this game, we are going to create several instances of extra functionality over the original tutorial that comes with the product.

By the end of the process, you will have created a game, and you'll have a good idea how to use TGF2 to make your own game concepts. You will also have a good grounding, which will help you be ready to move on to other game genres.

Setting the Scene

FIRST, WE WILL NEED to create our blank game structure, which, in this case, is a three-frame game. The first frame will be our menu, the second will be our game, and the third will be our high scores frame.

We will call our three frames:

▶ **Main Menu**

▶ **Game Level 1**

▶ **End Screen**

Game Assets for ChocoBreak

The game graphics and objects have already been created for this game. In your own games, you may end up using some graphics off the full version CD or creating your own. You may even use a combination of prebuilt and new content.

Preparing Our Game

We first need to create our game file, or, as it's called in TGF2, our application file. Click on the New button or use the File > New option. You will now have an application file and a single frame.

In total, we are going to have three frames, but at the moment we only have one. We need to create two more:

1. Ensure that you are in the Storyboard Editor. Then click twice on the number opposite the More text box to add two more frames.

2. You should now have three frames, so let's rename them and name the application.

3. Right-click on the text Frame 1 in the Workspace toolbar and select Rename from the popup menu. Then type in the text "Main Menu" and press Return.

4. Right-click on the text Frame 2, select Rename, and type in "Game Level 1"; then press Return.

5. Finally, right-click on the text Frame 3, select Rename, type in the text "End Screen," and press Return.

6. Now we will rename the application. Right-click on the text Application 1 in the Workspace toolbar and then type "ChocoBreak."

7. You will see the results of this work in Figure 8.1.

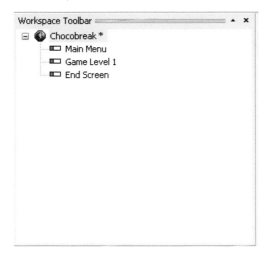

Figure 8.1
The frames created and renamed.

Connecting to the Prebuilt Library

You are nearly ready to start placing your graphics onscreen, but first you will need to get access to them. If you have the Library toolbar in the bottom of the TGF2 application, you will not need to do step one.

Let's display the Library toolbar, and then connect to the library for ChocoBreak:

1. First, let's display the Library toolbar, if it currently isn't displayed. Click on the View menu option, and then select Toolbars > Library Window. The Library toolbar window will appear.

2. In the left windowpane, you will see the words Local Library, next to a plus (+) sign. The plus sign means that you can click on it to expand the Local Library folder. Click on it once.

3. You will see the word Tutorials appear under the Local Library heading. Click on the word Tutorials.

4. Now the words ChocoBreak Tutorial appear in the right pane of the Library toolbar. Double-click on the words ChocoBreak Tutorial to display all the graphics we can use in the game we are about to make. You can see the library of graphics that will be used in Figure 8.2.

Figure 8.2
Graphics available in the ChocoBreak tutorial.

Library Files

You can create your own library files that can be accessed through the Library toolbar. All library files are made in TGF2 and saved as standard MFA files. Place them in a folder. You then can right-click on the left pane of the Library toolbar to create a new connection, and then point to the folder where your MFA file is stored and name your library. This is a great way of accessing common objects that you might want in your games.

Preparing the Main Menu

The first thing we need to do with our game is to place all of the objects onscreen. The first screen we will configure is the Main Menu. This is the frame that is used as the program's starting point, and you will be able to move from this screen to the game.

The Main Menu is a simple frame with a single background image. So let's first go to the frame editor of the correct frame and set up the single graphic on the screen.

1. We need to get on the Main Menu frame. Double-click on the Main Menu text in the Workspace toolbar or click on the number 1 in the Storyboard Editor to access the first frame.

2. You should now see the blank frame. Click on the object "ScreenTitle" in the Library toolbar, keep the left mouse button pressed, and drag the object over the frame. Release the left mouse button, and the graphic will appear on the screen.

3. The graphic is most likely not centered correctly. Right-click on it and select Align in Frame>Horz Center. This will move the object to the left or right so it is in the correct position. Right-click again and this time select Align in Frame>Vert Center. This will move the object up or down so that it correctly fits the frame.

4. Your frame will now resemble Figure 8.3.

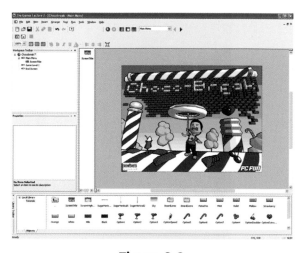

Figure 8.3
The ScreenTitle placed on the frame.

Positioning an Object

There are three ways to position an object. Where you want the object to appear on the screen will depend on which method is best to use. You can use:

Center: If the image, as in the case of the main menu, is the same size as the frame, then you just want to position it at the center vertically and horizontally. This will cover the whole frame precisely. To do this, you right-click on the object and select Align in Frame>Horz Center and Align in Frame>Vert Center.

Exact coordinates: If you want to place an object at a particular position on the screen, you can type in the X and Y coordinates. To do this, click on the object that is currently on the frame (which in this case is the ScreenTitle object). You will see the object properties window filled with information. Click on the Size/Position tab within this property window. You can then put in the exact location coordinates. For a graphic that is the same size as the frame, you can type in 0 for both coordinates.

Precise movement: If you have placed an object onscreen and you want to move it a couple of pixels in any one direction, you have the cursor keys. The cursor keys (also called the arrow keys) allow you to move it in any one of four directions with each key press. Each key press will move the object a single pixel position in the direction of the key you have pressed. Before you press the cursor keys, you must ensure that the object has been selected by clicking on it.

Preparing Level 1

In this game, we have a single level game. In your own games, you might also have a single level or many levels. Setting up the levels is the same process as setting up the Main Menu frame, by dragging and dropping your objects onscreen. There is an additional step that you will need to do to create all the bricks in the game, which, you will recall from Chapter 2, is the aim of the game. We will come to this shortly.

We will need to be on the correct frame, and then we will need to get the main components onto the frame.

Object Coordinates

We have specified the coordinates of each particular object that we place onscreen within the following instructions so you can position them in the same location. You can also just place them in the relative position and the game will still work.

1. Double-click on the text "Game Level 1" in the Workspace toolbar to display the blank second frame of our game.

2. Let's first place the background sky image onto the frame. Drag and drop the Sky object from the Library toolbar and place it anywhere on the Game Level 1 frame. You may need to click the right mouse button on the object and use the Align in Frame option to center it perfectly (X0 and Y0).

3. We now will place the area in which the ball can bounce around. Drag and drop the object called SugarHorizontal, and place it in the top center of the frame (X321 and Y47).

4. Take the SugarVertical1 object and place it on the left side of the frame (X71 and Y264).

5. Drag and drop the SugarVertical2 object and place it on the right side of the frame (X572 and Y264).

6. Now we need to place the bat and ball, so place the Player object at the center bottom of the frame (Player at X317 and Y425). Drag the BallGolden to the frame above the Player object (X319 and 357).

Your frame will now look like Figure 8.4.

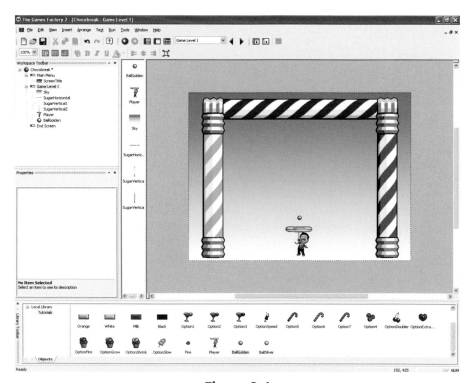

Figure 8.4
The Game Level 1 frame with most of the objects in place.

Creating Our Bricks

In our game, we want a set of bricks that the ball can hit and destroy. There are a couple of ways we could add the bricks. First, we could add them individually, but this is a laborious process, especially in this case where you must add 48 bricks. Alternatively, you can use the duplicate option, which will allow you to copy an object and replicate it a number of times on the frame.

We will now create our selection of boxes:

1. First, we need to place one brick onto the frame. Drag the White brick from the Library and drop it on the frame. Its position on the frame should be 145 for the X coordinate and 113 for Y.

2. To duplicate, right-click on the object, and the popup menu will appear. Select Duplicate.

3. The Duplicate dialog box, shown in Figure 8.5, will appear. This dialog box allows you to specify how many rows and columns of an object to create, and also how much space you want between each object.

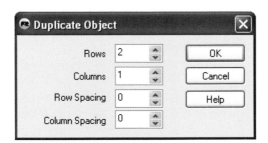

Figure 8.5
The Duplicate Object dialog box.

4. In the Rows box, type in the number 4, and in the Columns box type in 12. This will create a selection of bricks across the frame, as shown in Figure 8.6.

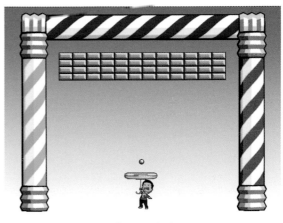

Figure 8.6
The frame with the selection of bricks all placed onscreen.

Object Naming

When you use the Duplicate option, TGF2 will automatically create the new object on the frame with the same name as the copied object. When you use cloning, TGF2 will take the original name and add the next chronological number to the end of it. So if you have an object called Brick, the next cloned object name will be called Brick2, then Brick3, and so on.

Duplicate Versus Clone

There are two ways of making multiple versions of the same object. For the ChocoBreak game, you have used the Duplicate option, but there is also the Clone object. Again, this is accessible from the popup menu when right-clicking on the object. There is a big difference when using these two options, although from first use they seem to have the same result. Duplicate creates copies of an image, which are all accessible via a single object in the Event Editor. Cloning will create a brand new object, and this will be represented by a separate object in the Event Editor. In our ChocoBreak game, we will check to determine when the ball has hit a brick, and if we used Duplicate, we only need to do a single check to see whether the ball has collided with the White brick. TGF2 will then check which duplicate brick the ball has collided with, and any actions for that event will only apply to that brick. If we cloned, we would have to create a number of events to check which brick was collided with. This would be a lot of work; in this game, it would mean 48 events just to check for a collision between the ball and each individual brick.

Configuring the Objects

Before we leave the Game Level 1 screen and move on to the last screen, there is one final bit of configuration that we need to do. We need to set up the properties on the ball and the bat so that they have their movement applied to them. This will allow you to move on to the logic programming of the game. The ball is going to use ball movement, and the bat (the spinning player graphic) will have mouse movement applied to it.

Let's configure the movement:

1. Click on the BallGolden object. This will display its properties in the Properties window. Click on the Movement tab in the Properties window to access the BallGolden movement properties. Currently, the movement is set to static, so click on the word Static (opposite the Type text) and from the drop down box, choose Bouncing Ball.

2. We want the BallGolden to fly initially only in an upward direction. Otherwise, the game might be very difficult if the ball flew in a downward direction as soon as the game frame has started. So click on the numbers opposite the Initial Direction text. A dialog box with arrows appears, showing that currently the ball can fly in any of the 32 directions. Click on the icon in the bottom right corner of the box to remove all the arrows. Click on some of the squares in an upward direction. You can see an example of this in Figure 8.7. The ball is now configured.

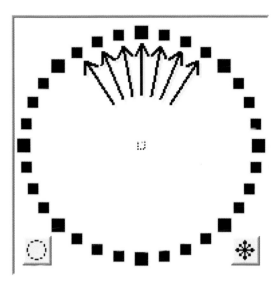

Figure 8.7
Configuring the ball's initial direction to upwards only.

3. To give the Player character the mouse movement, click on the Player object to access the player's properties. Because we were just in the Movement tab for a previous object, it will automatically be selected for this object. Click on the Static text, and from the drop down menu choose Mouse Controlled.

4. We need to configure the Mouse Controlled movement so that the player only moves between the two vertical sugar bars, so click on the Edit button opposite the Edit movement text in the Properties window. A dotted lined box will appear around the Player object. Move it so it covers most of the area between the bars as shown in Figure 8.8.

5. Click on the OK button in the Mouse Movement dialog box.

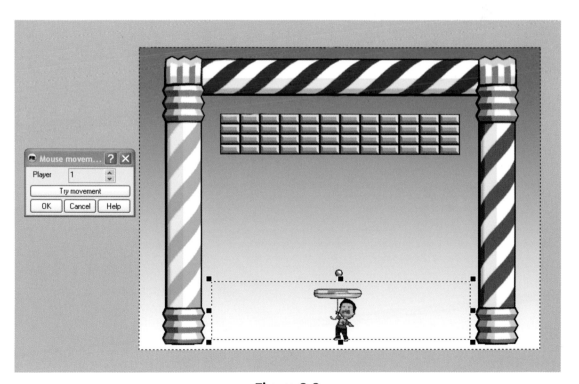

Figure 8.8
The mouse-controlled area where the player will be able to move.

Preparing the End Screen

Now you will need to set all the objects in place for the final screen—the End Screen. For this screen, we will also be placing a high scores table using the Insert Object option.

Let's move to the correct frame, add the background image, and then insert an object for the high scores table.

1. Double-click on the text End Screen in the Workspace toolbar to display the blank third frame.

2. Drag and drop the object ScreenHighscores to the frame.

3. Right-click on the object and use the Align in Frame>Horz Center and the Align in Frame>Vert Center to position it in the correct location.

4. Right-click anywhere on the frame area to see the popup menu and select Insert Object. The Create New Object dialog box will appear. Ensure that you select the Hi-score object and then click on OK.

5. The mouse cursor will change to a crosshair. Click anywhere in the center of the frame to place the object. We want to change the size of the Hi-score object to fit in better with our game, so ensure that it is selected, and then in the object properties, click on the Size position tab.

6. Change X coordinate to 165, Y coordinate to 206, width to 307, and height to 229. You can see this information in Figure 8.9.

Your final setup for the End Screen will look like Figure 8.10.

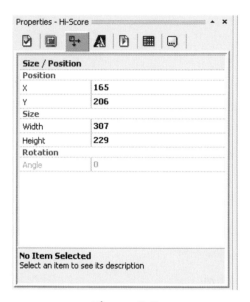

Figure 8.9
The Hi-scores object properties for its size and position.

Figure 8.10
The final layout of the End Screen.

Programming the Main Menu

NOW THAT YOU HAVE ALL of the scenes set for your game, it is time to begin programming them. We will start with the first frame, which is the first of our three frames. We only need to create a few events for this frame. First we will create a comment, then play some music, and finally, we will check for when the player presses the spacebar to make the game move to the Game Level 1 frame.

First, we need to ensure that we are on the correct frame before we access the Event Editor. Then we will add our first event, which will be a comment line about the game.

1. Double-click on the text Main Menu in the Workspace toolbar. This will display the first frame graphics that you set up earlier.

2. Click on the Event Editor button to display the blank sheet.

3. Now to add a comment: Right-click on the number 1 and select Insert>A comment. In the Comment dialog box, type in the following: "Picture Yourself Creating Games." Then press Return twice, and type in "ChocoBreak Version 1."

4. Click on the Centered radio button in the Alignment section.

5. Click on the Choose Font button, then select the Size of 16, and click on the OK button.

6. Click on the Set back color button, and then choose any light color from the color palette. In this example, we have selected the color yellow from the second row, second column. Once you have chosen your color, click on OK.

7. You will be back at the Edit text box. Click on OK to save this information to the Event Editor. You will see our comment line in Figure 8.11.

Notes and Colors

Many users find using comments and colors is a great way of making notes about their code. This is particularly useful if you have something complicated, so if you come back to it at a later stage, you will be able to understand. You can store text and numbers in TGF2 against particular slots, which are referenced by a number or name, so making a note of which parts of the program are writing to these slots is very helpful and will save you lots of time in the long run.

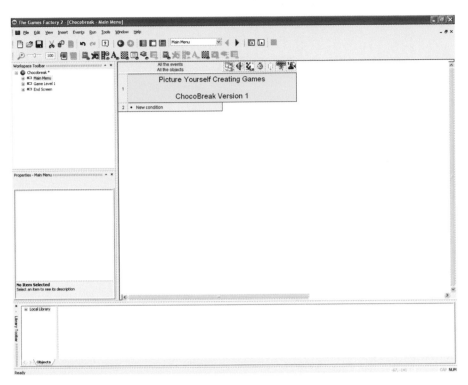

Figure 8.11
The first event line is our game comment.

The next event we will need to create is to play some music when the frame first loads. We can do this using the Start of Frame condition. We will tell TGF2 to play some music, as this is something that will make the Main Menu frame more enjoyable to the player.

Let's add our first event and action:

1. Click on the New Condition text on event line 2. When the New Condition dialog box appears, right-click on the Storyboard Controls object (the knight and chessboard icon), and from the popup menu, select Start of Frame. This condition will be added to the second event line.

2. Now you need to add the action; in this case, you want to play a song when the frame starts. To accomplish this, you need to right-click on the blank action box on event line 2, which is directly under the Sound object (the icon looks like a speaker). From here, two options will appear in a popup menu: samples or music. We want the Samples option, so select that, and then select the option Play Sample.

3. A Play Sample dialog box will appear, as shown in Figure 8.12; this allows you to search for a file on your computer, or in this case, on the CD-ROM that accompanies this book. So click on the Browse button that is next to the From a file text.

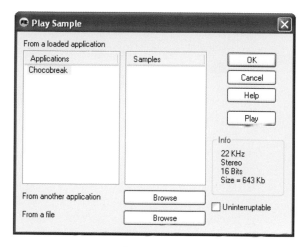

Figure 8.12
The Play Sample dialog box.

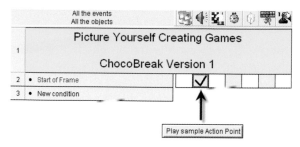

Figure 8.13
The Start of Frame event and its single action.

4. You now have an open dialog box, which allows you to browse for a particular sound file, and in this case a WAV file. Browse to your CD-ROM drive where the CD-ROM from this book is located, and go into the Game folder. You will see a file called Action Point.wav. Select this file and click on Open.

You will now see the action added to the Event Editor as shown in Figure 8.13.

Start of Frame

Even though this condition will only run at the very beginning of the frame, any actions can run for the life of the frame.

Samples and Music

In TGF2, the program differentiates between certain types of sound files. A sample is considered a WAV formatted file, while music is MIDI. WAV is a standard sound format on computers and is used in many aspects of the PC's operating system, including playing a short tune when logging in and beeping when there is an error. MIDI is quite an old sound format and although it is supported in TGF2, we don't recommend using it because it can create a pause between your program loading and the file actually being played.

Now it's time to add our next event, which will contain a single condition that will test for the player pressing the spacebar. When the player presses the spacebar, we will create an action to tell the game to go to the second screen.

1. First let's add the condition for the checking of the keyboard. Click on the New Condition text on event line 3. When the Object dialog box appears, right-click the Mouse Pointer and Keyboard object (its icon is a mouse and keyboard). From the popup menu, choose The Keyboard>Upon pressing a key. A dialog box will appear as shown in Figure 8.14, which is awaiting your key press. Press the spacebar, and the information will then be written to the Event Editor.

Figure 8.14
The dialog box awaiting a key press.

2. We have our condition, so now we need our action. The action is to move to the next frame, and to do this, we need to move across to the right until we are directly under the Storyboard Controls object. Right-click the action box and select Next Frame. You can see your action and event in Figure 8.15.

3. Well done, you have now completed the first screen in your game; you can test it by pressing the Run Application button or the F8 key. You will notice that the menu screen appears and plays some music (once), and if you press the spacebar, it will move to the game screen.

4. Quit the running game by pressing the red X in the top right corner, or alternatively press the Alt+F4 keys.

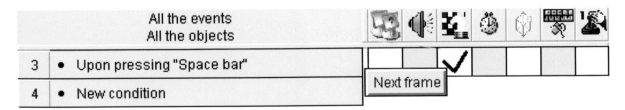

Figure 8.15
The condition and action on event line 3.

Programming Game Level 1

The game is the most important part of our three screens because this is where all of the action is going to take place. You may recall back in Chapter 2 where we discussed what would happen within our game and the features we wanted to include. We will now be adding some of these features into the game to create our first level.

Some of the things we need to do are:

► **Checking for the ball colliding with our Sugar bars, then telling it to bounce.**

► **Checking for the ball colliding with the bat, then telling it to bounce.**

► **Checking for the ball leaving the play area at the bottom.**

► **Checking for the ball colliding with the bricks.**

Let's go to the correct frame, so we can then access the Event Editor for that frame. We will then start with our basic events to create the logic for our game:

1. First let's get to the right frame. Double-click on the Game Level 1 text in the Workspace toolbar. This will display the ball, bat, and bricks.

2. Click on the Event Editor button on the toolbar to go to the events for this frame. You will go to the Event Editor and see only a single line with New Condition. This is now ready for you to begin creating the logic for the game.

3. We will create an event that will check for a collision between the ball and the left side sugar stick. Click on the New Condition text, and from the New Condition dialog box, right-click on the BallGolden object; this is the object we want to test. Then from the popup menu, select Collisions>With another object. Another dialog box will appear; select the SugarVertical1 object and click on OK.

4. Now we need the action; in this case, when the ball hits the sugar stick, we want the ball to bounce. Move to the right of the event line until you are directly under the ball, right-click the blank action box, and select Movement>Bounce. You can see the event and action in Figure 8.16.

5. We need to replicate the same events and conditions so that we check for a collision between the BallGolden and the SugarVeritcal2, and the BallGolden and SugarHorizontal. The actions for each of these three items will be that the BallGolden will bounce.

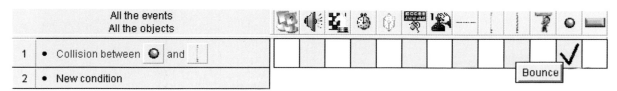

Figure 8.16
The first event and action for the Game Level 1 frame.

6. Next, do the same process, but this time check for a collision between the BallGolden and the Player object. Again move across to the right, until you are under the BallGolden object, and then set the Movement>Bounce.

7. Once you have done this, your actions and events will look like Figure 8.17.

8. You can run this frame of the program by pressing F7. Or, alternatively, press F8 to run the whole application and test the main menu also.

Exiting the Game Level 1 Frame

Remember that you will need to use the Alt and F4 key to exit the Game Level 1 frame because the mouse is tied to the player object.

Ball Going Out of Play

You will notice by running the game that the ball bounces around the screen off the sugar sticks and also bounces off the player's bat. Already, with only four events, you have a working game. Now we need to make it a little more fun and a little better at handling other events. For example, the ball can currently leave the bottom of the screen, and the game continues to play. This is not good for the player because all he can do at this point is move the bat around the screen.

We will now check when the ball has left the bottom of the screen. Once it has, we will end the game.

1. Click on the New Condition text on event line 5. We need to check for the BallGolden's position on the screen, so right-click the BallGolden object. From the popup menu, select Position>Test position of BallGolden.

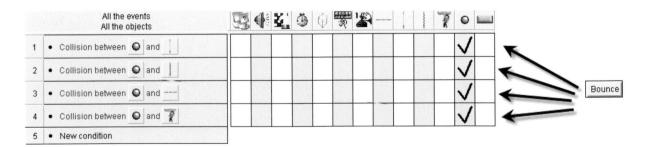

Figure 8.17
The four events that check for the collision between the ball and the game objects.

A new dialog box will appear as shown in Figure 8.18. This dialog box allows you to specify where the object (in this case, BallGolden) leaves or enters the screen. Click on the arrow that is pointing downward (at the bottom of the white box area called the frame area). If you are unsure which arrow to click, you can hold your mouse over the arrow and a text message will appear advising you what the graphic means. The arrow you need to select is called Leaves in the Bottom. Once this is selected, click on OK.

2. The event condition for line 5 will read "BallGolden leaves the play area on the bottom." We need to end the game when this is true, and we do that by moving to the next frame. Move across to the right until you are directly under the Storyboard Controls object, right-click, and select Next Frame.

3. Test the game and notice that once the ball has gone out of play, you are taken to the End Screen.

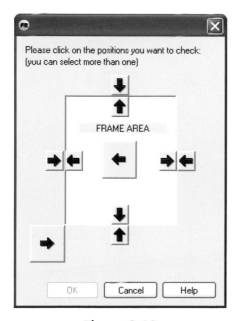

Figure 8.18
The testing of an object's position onscreen.

Test Position of an Object

The test position option allows you to check the current location of an object within the game. In the ChocoBreak example, this was to test that the ball was leaving the bottom of the screen. In other games, you might want to use some of the other options. This includes testing whether the object is leaving the top, bottom, left, or right of the screen by clicking on any of the small outpointing arrows. The large arrow in the middle checks to see if the object is currently in the frame play area. You can also test to determine if an object is coming into the frame by clicking one of the small arrows pointing inwards for the particular direction (top, left, and so on). Finally, you can also test to see if an object is outside the frame by clicking on the large arrow in the bottom left of the dialog box.

Destroying the Bricks

To give the player a challenge, but also to have something that we can register a score against, we need to destroy the bricks once they have been hit by the ball. If you think about this logically, the condition you will need is to check for a collision between the BallGolden and the White brick.

We will now add this condition and the actions that will be needed to destroy the White brick, and we will also add 20 to the score.

1. Click on the New Condition text on event line 6. When the dialog box appears, right-click on the BallGolden object. From the popup menu, choose Collisions>Another object. The Test a collision dialog box appears. Select the White brick object and click on OK. The event is now added.

2. Next we will add to the score, so move across to the right of event line 6 until you are directly under the Player1 object. This object's icon is a joystick and a hand. Right-click on the blank action box and select Score>Add to score. The Expression Evaluator will appear, so type in 20, as shown in Figure 18.19, and then click on OK.

3. Still on event line 6, move across until you are directly under the GoldenBall icon, right-click, and select Movement>Bounce.

4. Again on event line 6, move across until you are under the White brick object, right-click the action box, and select Destroy. You will see the event and its actions in Figure 8.20.

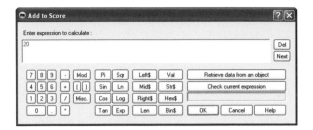

Figure 8.19
Expression Evaluator with the score of 20 added.

The Score

Even though we won't have anything onscreen displaying the score, TGF2 will keep track of the score in the background. If it finds that the score obtained once the game goes to the End Screen is higher than those on the high scores table, it will ask the user for her name and then add it to the board results.

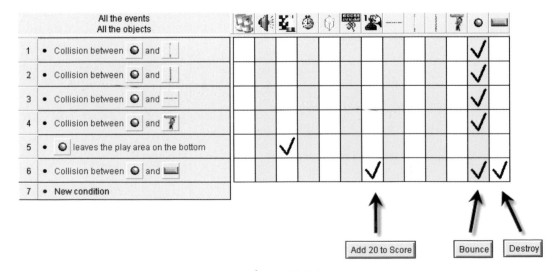

Figure 8.20
The condition and actions for event line 6.

Destroying Bricks

You can configure your games differently by just changing a single action. In this case, we told the ball to bounce when it hit a brick. It would then destroy that brick. This creates a situation where the ball only destroys one brick at a time. If we removed the bounce action, the ball would go through the bricks in its path and destroy them.

Run the game now and you will see that when the BallGolden hits a White brick, it will bounce off it, but the brick will be destroyed. If the player is really good at the game and destroys all of the bricks, currently there would be no result. So we need to add a condition that will check to see if all White bricks have been destroyed and, if so, move to the next frame.

Let's now add this new event:

1. Click on the New Condition text in event line 7. Right-click the White bricks object, then select Pick or Count>Have all White been destroyed. This will then create a new condition, which will continue to test until the final White brick has been destroyed. After the condition is met, the actions will be run.

2. Move to the right until you are directly under the Storyboard Controls object and then select Next Frame.

Adding Sounds

At the moment, our Game Level 1 frame is missing one vital ingredient, and that is sound. If you play the game without sound, it doesn't feel complete. It is very important to add sound to make the game more fun to play. We don't need to add any additional events to put our sound actions against; we can use those that we have already created.

First we will create a sound against the BallGolden colliding with SugarVertical1, SugarVertical2, and SugarHorizontal.

1. Our very first event is a collision between the BallGolden and SugarVertical1. Move across this event line until you are directly under the Sound object. Right-click the blank action box and select Samples>Play Sample. When the dialog box appears, click on the Browse button opposite the From a file text, and locate the Game folder on the CD-ROM. Select the file called impact02.wav and click on Open.

2. You can now do the same action using the same method for event lines 2 and 3, or you can drag and drop the check mark in the action box for event line 1 into the corresponding action boxes below it. You will see the result of putting this sound action into the other two events in Figure 8.21.

3. We want a sound when the BallGolden collides with the White brick, so move across from event line 6, right-click on the Sound icon, Samples>Play Sample, and then browse for a file. Select the pop04.wav file.

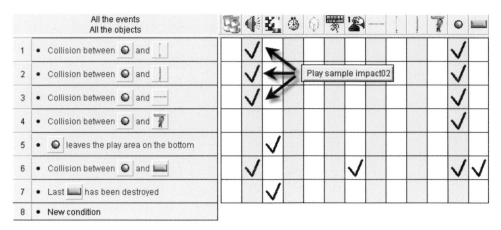

	All the events / All the objects													
1	• Collision between O and |		✓										✓	
2	• Collision between O and |		✓	Play sample impact02									✓	
3	• Collision between O and ---		✓										✓	
4	• Collision between O and 🏃												✓	
5	• O leaves the play area on the bottom			✓										
6	• Collision between O and ▭	✓					✓						✓	✓
7	• Last ▭ has been destroyed			✓										
8	• New condition													

Figure 8.21
The actions in all three events.

Automatic High Scores Dialog

If you run the game now, you will see that you can play the game and destroy the bricks, and if you let the ball go off the bottom of the screen, the game will go to the End Screen. You may also notice that in some cases it might ask you for your name as shown in Figure 8.22. This is because we have a Hi-score object on the last screen, and by default, this will check any score contained within TGF2 against the table when the frame is loaded.

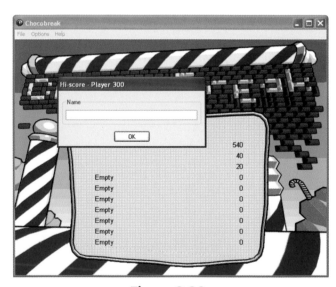

Figure 8.22
The Hi-score object finds that the player has scored a new high score and asks the player for his name.

Programming the End Screen

The final frame of our game is the End Screen. This is where you show the player all of the current scores and enter a high score if she obtains it. There are only two things we need to do on this screen. These include:

▶ **Play music when entering the frame.**

▶ **Wait five seconds and then tell the program to restart the application.**

Difference Between Restarting the Application and Jumping to Frame

In this example, we restarted the application. This has a major benefit over using Jump to Frame that you need to remember when making your own games. Restarting the application clears all the scores and lives the player has obtained and effectively resets them. If you used Jump to Frame, the player's scores and lives would be retained. This means the player would only have to hit a small number of bricks each time and her score would slowly increase. Restarting a frame is very useful if you want to repeat the same level over because this keeps the scores and lives as we mentioned. This is a very quick and easy way of making multiple levels of your games.

Let's make sure we are on the correct frame before we enter the Event Editor; then we will create our two events. The first will be a Start of Frame event because we want music to play as soon as the frame is entered and because we will do a timer event to check when the timer has reached five seconds before restarting the application.

1. Double-click on the text End Screen in the Workspace toolbar to display the final frame of our game. Then click on the Event Editor button, where you will then be taken to the blank events screen.

2. We will now create our first event for this frame. Click on the New Condition text on line 1 and then right-click on the Storyboard Controls icon and select Start of Frame. Move across to the Sound object and then right-click on the action box and select Samples> Play Sample. The Play Sample dialog box will appear, and you will notice that it lists all of the samples we previously used. We want to play the song that we used on the Main Menu screen, so all we need to do is select Action Point from the samples list and click on OK.

3. Now we will add the timed event. Click on the New Condition text on event line 2 and then right-click the Timer object; this object resembles a stopwatch. From the popup menu, select Is the timer equal to a certain value? A dialog box will appear, allowing you to select a timeframe in hours, minutes, and seconds. Change the 1 second to 5 seconds, either using the box where you can type the result or the slider bar. You can see how it should look in Figure 8.23. Once it is set to 5 seconds, click on the OK box to save this information to the event.

4. The condition will have been added, so now move across to the right until you are under the Storyboard Controls object, right-click the action box, and select Restart the Application.

If you now run the whole game, which you can do by pressing the F8 key or clicking on the Run Application button, you will be able to run through the whole game, try to get a high score and enter it on the score table. Finally after five seconds, the game will be completed.

Congratulations! You have completed your first game and are on your way to making your own fun and exciting games.

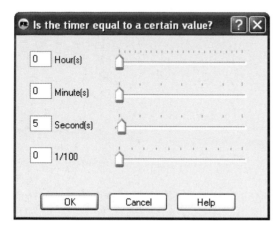

Figure 8.23
The timer dialog box where you specify a timeframe.

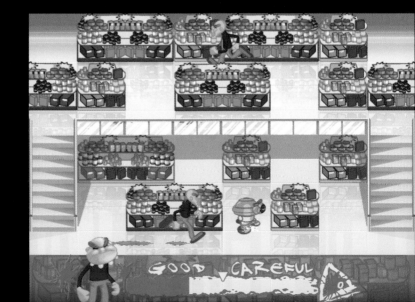

Adding More
Features

I N Chapter 8, you created a game called ChocoBreak. This game was a simple bat and ball game where you had to destroy the bricks to gain your points and the ultimate aim was to get on the high scores table. ChocoBreak is a lot of fun, but there is so much more that we could do with it by adding a few objects, making some configuration changes, and adding some new code. In this chapter, we will add some more features to ChocoBreak, which will take the game up another level.

In our game, we made changes that were necessary to get the game working; now we will see how we can improve the overall game and add other features that you come to expect in any typical computer game.

This chapter will build on what you have already learned and hopefully will give you an idea of how to improve your own games once they have been considered complete.

New Features

I F WE TAKE A LOOK at the current ChocoBreak game, there are several areas that could be improved, and that will increase the overall enjoyment for the player. At the moment the game is not using the concept of lives because it ends as soon as the ball leaves the screen. Additionally, there is no onscreen indication of how well you are doing score-wise. Finally, we will need to think about additional levels and other features.

The things we will be adding in this chapter include:

► **Add a score object to the screen so players can see how well they are doing.**

► **Add a lives object to the screen so players can see the lives they have.**

► **Change the code for the game level 1 frame to not exit when the ball goes out of the bottom of the screen.**

► **Change the code for game level 1 that removes a life when the ball exits from the bottom of the frame, then replace the ball back into the middle of the frame and remove one life.**

► **Check when there are no lives left, and if none are left, go to the End Screen.**

► **Configure the high scores table on the End screen to be more of a challenge for the player.**

► **Repeat the level or add a level.**

► **Create items that will fall for the player to catch which will add bonus items.**

Adding New Objects

We will first add a score object to keep track of the player's score and a lives object to display the number of lives the player has left. It is good to give the game player an indicator of how well she is doing because this gives her an idea of how far away she is from getting her next high score, which is one of the factors that will make someone want to replay your game.

Let's open the game file and continue with adding some new features:

1. Open TGF2. Click on File>Open, then browse to the CD-ROM that contains the CD from this book. Navigate to the Game folder, select chococomplete.mfa, and click on Open.

2. We need to be on the Game Level 1 frame to place our objects, so double-click on the Game Level 1 text in the Workspace toolbar. You will now see the game level 1 frame with the Player, White, and BallGolden objects.

3. Right-click anywhere on the frame and select Insert Object. From the dialog box that appears, select the Score object. Click anywhere on the frame to place it. Click on the Score object that is now somewhere on the frame, then access its Size/Position tab in the Properties toolbar and set its X coordinate to 166 and its Y coordinate to 470.

4. Right-click again anywhere on the frame and select Insert Object. From the selection of objects, choose the Lives object. Click anywhere on the frame to place the lives graphic, which is represented by three hearts. On the Size and Position tab for the lives object, ensure that the X coordinate is set to 471 and the Y coordinate to 445. You can see what the frame now looks like in Figure 9.1.

If you run the frame now by pressing F7, you will notice that the score will update automatically without your needing to write any additional code. This is because when you set the score to add 20 every time a brick is hit, TGF2 kept this score ready. As soon as you place the Score object, TGF2 knows that it needs to set the current score to the graphical object that is on the frame.

Lives

By default, the player has three lives. This is configured whenever you use the lives system. This is fine for our game. The lives starting number can be changed in the application properties or via an action in the Event Editor.

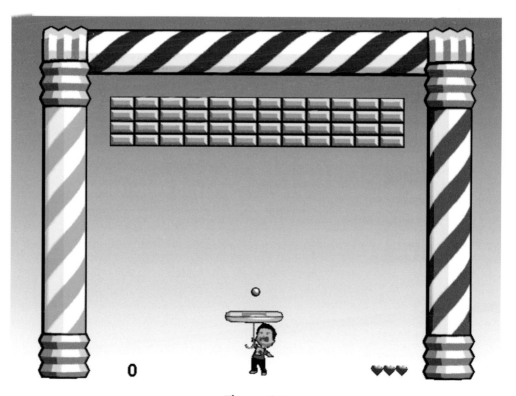

Figure 9.1
How the frame will look once you've added the two new objects.

Additional Event Editor Programming

We now need to make some changes to the Event Editor to update our game with these new features. When doing this in your own game, you may only have a few events or you may have many. It is sensible to make a small number of changes and then test your game to see how it is reacting. First, we need to be in the Event Editor for the Game Level 1 frame. So click on the Event Editor button.

Removing a Life

You will see the seven events that made up the original game frame. The first thing we will do is make a small change to the game to stop the game from ending when the ball has left the play area. This is a very simple change, and it just requires the deletion of an action. We will then create the action on the same event line to remove a life. In many cases, you can use already created conditions; you do not always need to create new ones.

1. Move across from event line 5 of the Game Level 1 frame and click on the action that is contained within the Storyboard Controls object. Press the Delete key to remove this action. This will not end the game when the ball leaves the bottom of the screen.

2. Now we need to add the action to reduce the lives by one, so on the same event line (5), move across until you are directly under the Player 1 object, right-click the action box, and select Number of Lives>Subtract from number of Lives. When the Expression Evaluator appears, type in the number 1 and click on OK. Now every time the ball goes off the screen, a life will be removed.

3. We also need to destroy the BallGolden after it has left the screen because we no longer need it. So move across on event line 5 until you are directly under BallGolden, right-click the action box, and select Destroy.

4. Finally, we need to create a new ball because we destroyed the one that went off screen. Still on event line 5, move across from the condition until you are under the Create object. Right-click and select Create Object. The Create Object dialog box appears as shown in Figure 9.2. Scroll down until you can see the BallGolden object. Select it because this is the one you want to create. Click on OK in the Create Object dialog box.

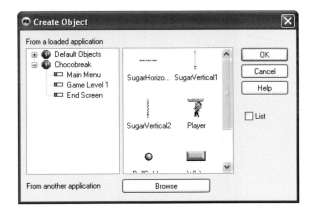

Figure 9.2
The Create Object dialog box.

5. You will now see a dialog box asking you where you want this new object to be created. Drag the box with the cross in it over the original BallGolden and then click on OK.

6. You can see the new actions and the order they were added in Figure 9.3.

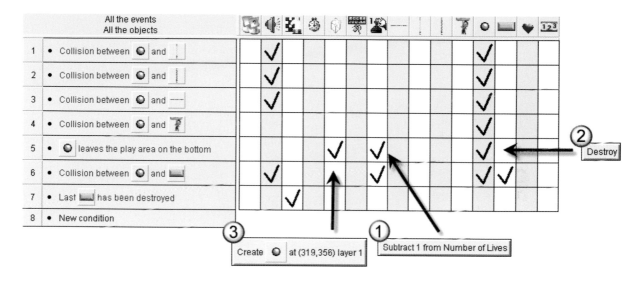

Figure 9.3
The new action to remove a life when the ball goes off the screen.

Order of Actions

It is very important to add the actions in the order that has been detailed previously; otherwise, you could experience problems with your game. For example, you could have programmed your game to create the ball before destroying it. If you had done this, as the ball is created and repositioned back onscreen, it would have then been destroyed. This would mean you wouldn't see any new ball.

Other Ways to Program

TGF2 is a very powerful program which allows you to achieve the same results using different code. Rather than destroy and recreate the ball, you could have repositioned it back on the screen. The benefit of destroying the ball and recreating it is that the ball will be reset and will move in an upward direction because that is how it is configured in the initial movement. If we just reposition it, the ball will continue to move downwards after it is repositioned. Of course, you could also code an action to tell the ball to move upwards. You can see that there are a number of ways of achieving the same result.

No Lives Left

If you play the game, you will notice that the ball can fly off screen and that a life will be removed and the ball repositioned back to its original spot, where it will move in an upward direction. You may also notice that you can lose all three lives and the game continues to play. We now need to add the condition and action to check when the player has no lives left.

This is a very straightforward process:

1. Click on the New Condition text on event line 8. We want to do a test on the number of lives, and this is stored under the Player 1 object, so right-click on it and select When number of lives reaches 0.

2. We now need to add the action, which in this case is to go to the next frame. Move to the right of this event until you are directly under the Storyboard Controls object, right-click the action box, and select Next Frame. You can see the event line and action in Figure 9.4.

Configuring the High Scores Table

When playing the game at the moment, the user doesn't have any challenge; as long as he hits a brick, he will get on the scoreboard. The default settings are set to the name Empty and the score of 0. When creating a game, you should consider how challenging the game is for the player. You should place a number of lower scores in the table to ensure that the player can relatively easily score enough points to get on the board. The scores should get progressively harder for the player to reach to give him a target to strive for, which ultimately will give your game more longevity.

You will now edit the high scores table to give the player more of a challenge:

1. First we need to be on the last frame, so double-click on the End Screen text in the Workspace toolbar.

2. You can see the high scores table with its 10 empty slots. Double-click on it to open up the Setup dialog box. You will see the 10 empty names and scores all set to zero.

3. Starting from the top, double-click any line to bring up the Edit dialog box, where you can then type in an entry. You can see the dialog box for the name if you double-click the empty text in Figure 9.5.

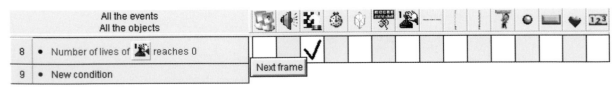

Figure 9.4
Checking the number of lives and moving to the next frame.

Figure 9.5
The Hi-score object edit box used to edit a particular entry.

4. You will have to also double-click on the 0 to edit the number separately. You can see the dialog box with all the entries complete in Figure 9.6.

5. After you click on OK in the dialog box in Figure 9.6, the high scores table will be updated with the relevant entries.

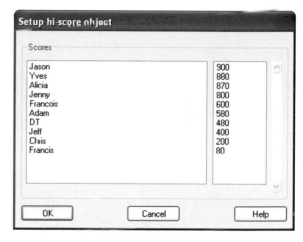

Figure 9.6
The final contents of the Hi-score object.

High Scores Table Updates

When you were testing the game, you may have entered your name. Even after entering a new set of score data, you will still see the old data and not the new entries you have just entered. This is because TGF2 checks to see if there is any data already in a file called an ini file, and if there is, it will not display this new data. The important thing to remember is that when you give the game to someone else, it will display the correct list that you entered manually. You do have another option if you want to see the data displayed when you run the game. You can click on the Hi-score object, and in the Settings tab, you can enter a file name to use for the ini file. This will create a brand new score file and will automatically display the information you entered.

Adding Additional Levels

At the moment, we have a single game level called Game Level 1, but what if you wanted to create many levels with varying difficulty and different items on each one? There are a number of ways you can achieve this goal.

Here are some ways of creating additional levels:

▶ **Copy and Paste: You can copy and paste whole frames and their Event Editor code to create new frames. You can do this using the Workspace toolbar or the Storyboard Editor, and then use the standard keyboard shortcuts to copy a frame, then paste it. You can then go into the frame and Event Editors for each of your pasted frames and make changes, and then you have your new levels.**

- ▶ **Restart Frame:** If you want a level to repeat over and over without needing to change anything, you don't need to make any additional levels. We already have a condition that checks for when all bricks have been destroyed. All you need to do is replace the action to jump to the next frame with a restart frame. This won't increase the complexity of the level, but in certain types of games where the difficultly level is already quite high, this allows a good player to score more points.

- ▶ **Brand New Frames:** If you are making a game where different levels will actually contain different graphics or game types, then you can create a new frame in the same way you would create a normal frame. Place all of your objects on the frame and then program it in the Event Editor. This is the slowest of the three options, and it is unlikely that you will create many games where the level does not use some of the graphics or code.

Creating Items That Will Fall

We are going to make another change to our game to show you how to add bonus items to the game. We will, at random, drop items from the bricks that the player can catch or avoid. This will make the game more complex for the player but also add another level of fun to it.

We will create an event so that every two seconds an object will fall from one of the bricks that still exist. To make sure we have enough time to play the game, we will also restart the level if all of the bricks have been destroyed.

The CD-ROM included with this book already contains the ChocoBreak game file ready to use; alternatively, if you have the ChocoBreak game still open from the previous chapter, you can also use that.

Let's load the file and begin to make our changes to the game:

1. Open TGF2, then click on File>Open from the menu options. Browse your computer and go to the CD-ROM drive that contains the book's CD. Navigate into the Game folder and select chococomplete2.mfa and click on Open.

2. We first need to add an object that will drop from the bricks onto the Frame Editor. We will need to be on the Game Level 1 frame, so double-click on the text Game Level 1 in the Workspace toolbar.

3. Expand the Local Library text in the Library toolbar, select Tutorials, and double-click on the ChocoBreak Tutorial text in the right-side windowpane. Look for the object called Option1 and drag it on to the frame. Place it to the left of the game window so that it does not appear onscreen. You can see a good location to put it in Figure 9.7. The location of this object is X −46 and Y 239.

Figure 9.7
The new object that will fall from our bricks, currently off screen.

4. We want to add a movement to the Option1 object, so on the Frame Editor, click on the object to bring up the object's properties. Click on the Movement tab, and then choose Bouncing Ball in the Type drop down menu. Click on the Initial direction numbers and remove all the arrows, and then place a single arrow pointing downward. This will mean that when the object appears in the game, it will move downward automatically. You can see the object movement properties in Figure 9.8.

5. Now we need to add some code, so enter the Event Editor for the Game Level 1 frame. First, we need to amend event line 7 where the last brick has been destroyed. Move across to the action under the Storyboard Controls object and delete it. Right-click on the now blank storyboard controls action box and select Restart the current Frame. This will now make the frame loop until the player has no lives left, at which time it will then go to the final frame.

Figure 9.8
The Option1 movement properties.

6. Let's now create the condition that will wait two seconds. Click on the New Condition text on event line 9, then select the Timer object. From the popup menu, choose Every. When the Timer dialog box appears, change the seconds number to two and click on OK.

7. We now need to add a second condition to the same event line to pick a White brick at random. So right-click on the text Every 02"-00 on event line 9 and from the popup, select Insert. The New Condition dialog box will appear. Right-click on the White brick object and then select Pick or Count>Pick White at Random. Now every two seconds, it will pick one of the bricks at random.

8. Move across from the conditions on event line 9 until you are under the Create New Objects object. Right-click on the action box and select Create Object. The Create Object dialog box appears. Scroll down until you find the Option1 object, select it, and click on OK. You will now be asked to position this newly created object, and there are a number of options. We could specify a particular position, but we want it to appear to come from one of the bricks. So click on the "Relative to" radio button and a dialog box will appear.

Choose the White brick object and click on OK. You can see this event and its action in Figure 9.9.

9. A further dialog box will appear as shown in Figure 9.10. You will also see that one of the White bricks is selected and is connected to a dotted line and dotted box. By moving this box, you can tell TGF2 where to create the object based on the position of the selected object. Because we used Duplicate, all of these White bricks are the same, so the position will be the same for any of the bricks. For example if you stated that the object's position was five pixels to the right of the object, then an object will always be created five pixels to the right of any of the White bricks. Move the dotted box or type in 0, 0 for the X and Y coordinates. This will place the creation of the Option1 object in the center of the brick. Click on OK to save this information to the Event Editor.

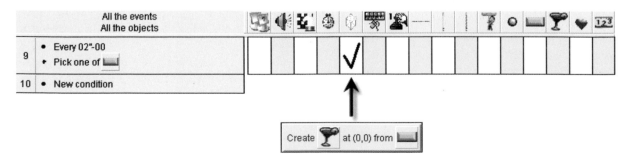

Figure 9.9
The conditions and actions for creating an object every two seconds at random.

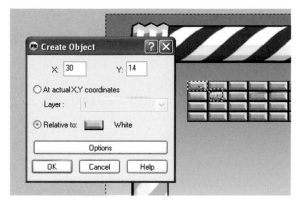

Figure 9.10
The location relative to the object.

Creating an Object from White Brick

You might wonder when you set the relative position to the White brick why the 0,0 coordinates were in the center of the object. This is because, within the object, the Action point is placed directly in the middle of the object.

If you now run the game, you can play it and every two seconds an object will fall from one of the White bricks at random. There are a number of things that you would now need to consider with this game. You will need to check for a collision between the object and the player object (the bat). Also, what action do you want to happen when it does hit, and finally, what happens if the player misses the Option1 object?

These are all things that can be configured in any way you want in your own games; for example, if the player catches the Option1 object, perhaps it adds an additional life or adds more to the score.

With objects flying off screen, it is always recommended that you destroy the objects once they have left the screen. This just makes your program a little more efficient. You won't notice any problems with a game as small as ChocoBreak, but if you were making a game with hundreds of objects flying off screen and you didn't delete these objects after they left the screen, you might find your game slowing down. This is because the computer needs to spend processor time and memory keeping track of the position and other properties of these no longer in use objects. Of course, in some games you will want objects to go off screen and then to fly back onscreen, and in that case, you wouldn't destroy that particular object.

Let's now create our additional code changes to check for a collision, add 30 points to the score when they catch an Option1 object, and destroy any objects if they are off screen.

1. First we will check for a collision. So click on the New Condition text and select the Player object (the bat). From the popup menu, choose Collisions>Another object, then select the Option1 object. Move across to the right until you are directly under the Player1 object (the joystick icon) and select Score>Add to score. In the Expression Evaluator, type in 30 and click on OK.

2. The second thing we need to do is check to see if the Option1 object leaves the bottom area of the screen. Click on the New Condition text, and select the Option1 object; then from the popup menu, choose Position>Test position of Option1. When the Position dialog box appears, click on the down pointing arrow in the bottom half of the dialog box and click on OK. Move across to the right of this event until you are directly under the Option1 action box, right-click, and select Destroy.

3. You can see the conditions and actions for this in Figure 9.11.

You might also want to destroy the option1 object once it collides with the player1 object. To do this, all you will need to do is find the event that contains the collision between player1 and option1, move across to the action box for the option1, and select Destroy.

Congratulations! You have finished your first game and added some new features along the way. Think about other ways you could improve your game. Perhaps you could add more falling objects that create different effects, for example, creating a second ball and removing a life.

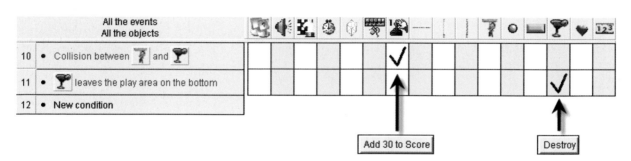

Figure 9.11
The final events for our game.

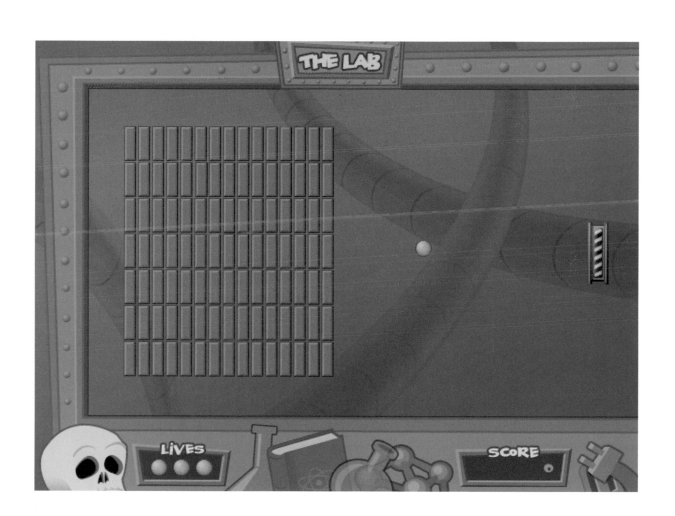

Reversi

Pass

Stop

Restart

Score
2

Score
2

Additional Program
Changes

WHEN MAKING YOUR OWN GAMES, you may want to configure the game to look a certain way. You might want to display a menu or remove the menu. You might want to display the game in a window or in full screen mode where it covers the whole desktop. TGF2 is very powerful and has many options available that you can configure to give your games a unique look and feel.

In this chapter, we will look at some of the options that are available to you and how they might affect how your game looks and plays.

Screen Changes

TGF2 ALLOWS YOU TO CHANGE many aspects of the screen size. We have already talked about the frame and application sizes in Chapter 3. Now we will look at some other screen changes that you might require.

Full Screen

You may have noticed when playing games that often the screen resolution changes and the game takes over the whole screen. The Windows Start bar is covered and no part of the desktop is shown. This is called full screen, and it resizes the games frame size to match the screen size.

To change your game to use this settings do the following:

1. Open TGF2 and load a game using the File>Open option.

2. Click on the application name in the Workspace properties toolbar to access the application properties sheet.

3. Click on the Window tab in the application properties sheet.

4. Scroll down and select the Change Resolution Mode checkbox as shown in Figure 10.1.

Figure 10.1
The Change Resolution option selected.

This checkbox is enough to change the program to take the whole screen. You can see an example of this process in the Examples folder on the CD-ROM. The file is called fullscreen.mfa. You will notice when running that file and any games that you set to full screen that there is a bar that appears on the top of the window.

This is the debugger bar, and it is used to check for bugs within your games. You can click on the X to close it for now. Behind the debugger bar, you will see a set of file menus. In most full screen games, you would create your own menus and not use the default one that is used in games that appear in a window. We will show you how to remove this shortly. You can see these items in Figure 10.2.

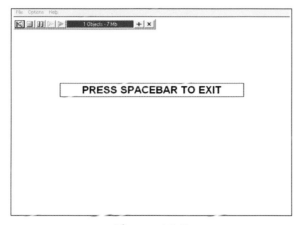

Figure 10.2
The debugger bar and the text menu on our full screen.

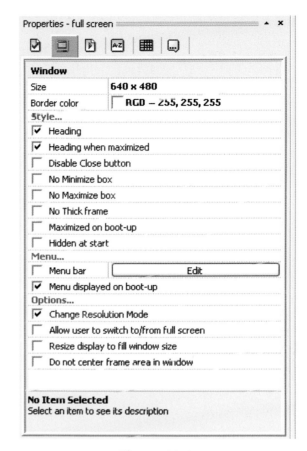

Figure 10.3
The Menu bar unchecked will remove the menu when running the game.

Removing a Menu

If you are working in full screen, you may want to remove the text menu that appears on the top of the screen. To do this:

1. With your file open, click on the application name to access the application properties.

2. Click on the Windows tab in the application properties window.

3. Unselect the Menu bar option as shown in Figure 10.3.

Removing the Menu When Running the Game

You may want to leave the menu and allow the player to display or hide it when required. The default key to hide the menu is F8.

Default Menu Options

Built into your games by default is a selection of menu options. These allow you to configure certain aspects of your game, ranging from changing the controls to accessing any help files and displaying the About box, which details copyright information. You can see an example of the default menu in Figure 10.4.

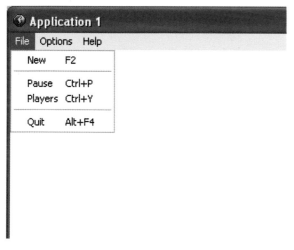

Figure 10.4
The default menu system provided by TGF2.

The basic menu contains three main headings, File, Options, and Help. These main headings contain the following:

File

▶ **New:** This starts the program afresh, thus causing the game to reload as if it was just started.

▶ **Password:** You can configure a password for a frame. By selecting this option and entering a password, you can make the program jump to a specific frame.

▶ **Pause:** This will pause the game in progress.

▶ **Players:** This configures the default player controls. This allows the player to change the controls of the game from keyboard to joystick (as many as four joysticks).

▶ **Quit:** This will exit the game.

Passwords Option

You can configure the passwords for each frame in the Storyboard Editor screen.

Password Option in Menu

The Password option in the menu will not appear unless you configure a password in the Storyboard Editor.

Options

▶ **Play Samples:** By default this is enabled, so any samples that are expected to play within the game will be heard on the speakers. Uncheck this, and no samples will be played.

▶ **Play Music:** This is the same as Play Samples, except that it applies to any music that will play within the game.

▶ **Hide the Menu:** If you don't want to see the menu while playing the game, you can hide it by selecting this option. It can be brought back by pressing the F8 key.

Help

▶ **Contents:** Disabled by default, Contents allows you to assign a Help file to the Menu option or shortcut key (a range of file formats including hlp, wri, and doc).

▶ **About:** When the user selects this, an information box details the product name and any copyright information.

Menu Dialog

It is very likely that you will want to change this default menu system to contain items that are more specific to your game. Many games create additional menu options to help navigate around the various screens of their programs. Games such as Railroad Tycoon and Civilization have many menu selections, which would not be easy to replicate onscreen using images and buttons. Using the in-game screen menus, users can quickly access some areas that would otherwise require two, three, or more clicks to reach.

To change the menu options used within your games, you will need to access the menu configuration dialog box, which is available via the application properties.

1. Start TGF2, click on the option File>New on the menu to create a new game file.

2. Click on the word Application 1 in the Workspace toolbar to bring up the properties sheet. On the application properties sheet, click the Window tab to bring up options relating to the menu. You should now see a properties sheet as shown in Figure 10.1.

3. Under the section Menu, you will see two checkboxes and an Edit button. If you wish to include a menu bar, you leave the Menu bar option selected, and if you would like the menu to appear when the game is started, the second option should be left at its default.

4. Click on the Edit button to open the Menu Editor. You will now see a menu dialog box as shown in Figure 10.5.

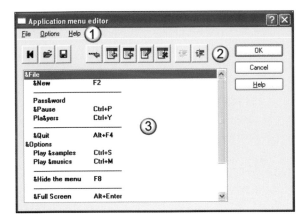

Figure 10.5
The Menu Editor dialog box is labeled as shown.

The parts of the Menu Editor dialog box shown in Figure 10.5 are as follows:

1. You can see an example of your text displayed automatically within the dialog box. It currently shows the File, Options, and Help menus. As you change your menu, this will be updated to reflect how it currently looks.

2. These are menu buttons that allow you to edit and change your menus. We will discuss each of these buttons shortly.

3. This is the actual structure of your menu, with its shortcut keys and any menu separations.

Shortcut Keys

Shortcut keys, also known as hot keys, are specific key combinations you can use that do the same thing as selecting the option from a menu. You may do this already when using your PC; for example, pressing Alt+F4 closes an application.

Dialog Buttons

The menu buttons consist of the following (from left to right):

- ▶ **Reset Menu: This will reset the menu back to its original settings after changes have been made.**

- ▶ **Load a Menu: This loads a menu from a file, allowing you to create an original menu and use it in multiple games without needing to recreate it each time.**

- ▶ **Save a Menu: This saves a menu so that it can be used at a later stage in the current or future programs.**

- ▶ **Insert a Separator: This creates a line separator between menu options. It is useful for grouping similar items together.**

- ▶ **Insert an Item: This allows you to create a menu text item.**

- ▶ **Insert an Item from the Default Menu: If you have created your own menu system but would like to take advantage of some of the default menu options, you can choose which ones to add.**

▶ **Edit Current Item:** Edit the currently selected line item (you will need to click on an item that you wish to be edited before clicking on this button).

▶ **Delete an Item:** Remove an item from the menu.

▶ **Push Left:** You can create various levels of menus, so that when one is selected, it will bring up another menu to the right of the selected option. This allows you to move the menu option higher or lower in the menu order.

▶ **Push Right:** You can move a menu item to the right of its current position using this button.

Editing a Menu Option

To edit a current menu option, you can either double-click on the item or single-click to highlight it and select the Edit current item button. Once you have done this, you will be presented with the Setup application menu dialog box, which can be seen in Figure 10.6.

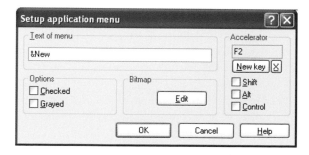

Figure 10.6
The Setup application menu dialog box for editing a menu option.

These options are:

▶ **Text of Menu:** Type in the text that you wish to appear in the menu system. By using an ampersand (&), you are telling TGF2 that it should underline the next available letter in the menu, so in this example the N would be underlined. This tells users that they can access this option using a shortcut key (a key combination that is configured under the Accelerator section).

▶ **Checked:** This places a check mark next to the word in the menu. This is useful for options that can be switched on or off (for example, in the default menu, the user can turn the music on and off).

▶ **Grayed:** A check in this box will gray out the option in the menu. When an item is grayed, it is effectively switched off and cannot be selected.

▶ **Bitmap:** By clicking on the Edit button, you will enter the Picture Editor and be able to create a button for your menu option. This allows users to create XP-based menus where many of the options have graphic images next to the menu text.

▶ **Accelerator:** This allows you to configure a shortcut key to a menu option. These are used in many types of games and applications to allow you to quickly access certain options. A default example would be quitting a TGF2 game by using the Alt key and F4 together to exit the program.

Menu Walkthrough

We are going to reconfigure the menu and add another main menu item alongside File, Options, and Help. This fourth entry will be called Book. Under the Book heading, we will create a number of entries, including one item with an image, a separator line, and two additional menus to create the menu in Figure 10.7.

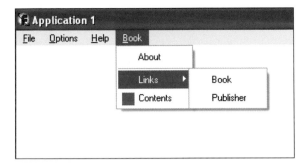

Figure 10.7
The menu that you will create.

1. Choose File>New option from the menu to create a brand new program file. Double-click on the text Frame 1 in the Workspace toolbar to open the Frame Editor.

2. Click on the word Application1 in the Workspace toolbar to bring up the properties sheet. On the application properties sheet, click the Window tab to bring up options relating to the menu.

3. Under the section Menu, click on the Edit box to begin changing the configuration of the menu.

4. Use the scrollbar to scroll downwards until you see a blank space below the word &About. Double-click on the blank line or click to highlight it and click on Insert an Item.

5. When the dialog box appears, type in &Book in the Text of Menu edit box, and then click on the OK button. Click on the Push Left button to move the Book item to the left; this will make it into its own menu option rather than an entry under Help.

6. Scroll down again, double-click on the blank line under the &Book entry, and type in the word About; then click on the OK button. On looking at the menu, you will notice that a new menu option has appeared and we wish it to be an item under &Book, so ensure the About entry is highlighted and then click on the Push Right button once to move it to the correct position.

7. Click on the blank line. Click on the Insert a Separator option to add a straight line under the About item.

8. Double-click on the blank line under the Separator item. Type in the text Links and click on the OK button.

9. Double-click on the blank line under the Links item and type in the text Book, then click on the OK button.

10. Double-click on the blank line under Book, type in the text Publisher, and click on the OK button.

11. We now need to move both the Book and Publisher items to the right of the Links item. Select the Book line (which is just below the Links line) by clicking on it. Then click on the Push Right button. Do the same process for the Publisher item.

12. Double-click on the blank line under Publisher, type in the text Contents, and then click on Edit button in the Bitmap section. You will now enter the Picture Editor, select the Fill Tool, and select a color. Fill the small square image with a single color and then click on the OK button. Then click on the OK button again to return to the Menu Editor. Ensure Contents is highlighted and then click on the Push Left button to place it in the correct sequence in the menu system.

13. Your menu is now completed. Click on OK to save the configuration of the menu to TGF2 (you will still need to save the game file to ensure that all changes are kept).

14. Ensure that you are on the Frame Editor, right-click on the frame, and select Insert Object. Choose the Formatted Text object and click on the frame. This will place the text object onscreen. You will see a box outline on the frame; double-click on it to make it editable. Type in some text within the box and then click off it to save the text to the object.

15. Click on the Formatted Text object again to access the object properties. Click on the Display options tab and then deselect the Visible at Start option so that it is unchecked.

16. Save the TGF2 file as Menu1.mfa; you will need to access this example shortly to program it within the Event Editor.

Using Menus

To utilize the menu you have just created, you will need to use the Event Editor to access its options and program how it should react to user selections.

Programming the Menu

If you want to make changes to the basic menu that is provided by default, you will need to create conditions and actions so that when a player selects a specific menu option the game will react in a certain way. All configuration of the menus is done via the Event Editor and via event code. When adding a condition, from the dialog box you would choose the Special object (the object that looks like two computers connected to each other); then from the popup menu, you would choose the Application menu to pick relevant conditions for what you want to be tested. In the following walkthrough, we are going to use the menu we have just created and create a condition that when the player selects Book>About, the game will display some text.

1. Using the file created in the Menu Walkthrough, open the file called Menu1.mfa.

2. Double-click on the text Frame 1 in the Workspace toolbar to open the Frame Editor. Click on the Event Editor button to begin programming the menu system.

3. Click on the New Condition text to open the New Condition dialog box. Right-click on the Special object and choose Has an option been selected? from the popup menu. You will now see a dialog box as shown in Figure 10.8.

4. Click on the Click Here button to see the already created menu, and choose Book>About. You will now see an event that says Menu option About selected.

5. Move to the right of the event until you are directly under the Formatted Text object, right-click, and choose Visibility, Make object Reappear from the popup menu.

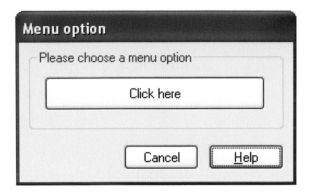

Figure 10.8
Menu option selector.

Icons

WHEN YOU RUN A GAME within an application window, or look at the executable of any game you have made by browsing the folder it is stored in, you will see a graphic icon. These icons are specially created to give the game individuality from others that are on your machine, as shown in Figure 10.9. The image on the left in Figure 10.9 is the graphic image you will see if you search for the program using Windows Explorer. The icon image on the right can be seen on the top left corner of the application window. There is a default set of icons pre-made within TGF2, which can be changed to better represent your games.

To amend these icons:

1. In the Workspace Properties toolbar, click on the topmost object (icon) to reveal the application properties in the properties tab.

2. Click on the About tab in the Properties toolbar.

3. Click on the line that represents Icon, and then click on the Edit box that appears.

The Picture Editor appears with four icons that can be amended. You can see an example of the icons used in the final version of a game in Figure 10.10.

Figure 10.9
An example of two icons that are displayed.

Figure 10.10
Example of the icons being amended.

Icons

You will notice in Figure 10.10 that there are a number of icons. There are a variety of sizes and colors. The icon used will depend on the screen resolution.

Pick 3 Sweets

OK

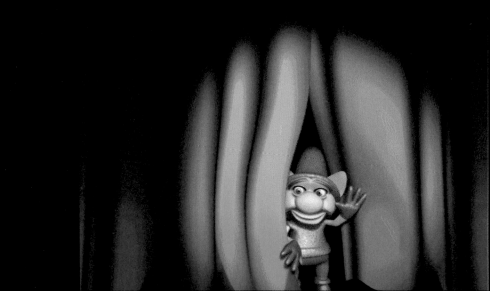

Distribution

YOU HAVE MADE YOUR GAME, but now what? Well, you might want to pass it to your friends to play, or perhaps you want to place it on the Internet so that users can download the game or even play it online. TGF2 has a number of different options available to the game creator to help you distribute your games.

Thanks to the Internet, there are many more ways of delivering your games and giving you access to a wider audience. There is still the challenge of making all these new users aware of your game on the Internet, but the potential is great.

In this chapter, we will look at how to create a single Windows executable file that can be played on any Windows machine. Unfortunately, you cannot e-mail executable files; programs like Outlook generally remove them because they consider executables to be potential viruses. Therefore, we will also explain how to place your game file into a zip file. This is a specially formatted file that is supported by Windows and that places one or many files into a single named file.

We will look at creating an installer for your game. This is very useful if you intend to use external graphics and sounds. The installer helps you easily place these files on the end user's PC, so that she doesn't need to worry about which files she needs to copy to which folder to get the game to work.

Finally, we will look at how you can place your games in a web browser using TGF's own web plug-in called Vitalize, which creates a file in a special format called CCN that can then be uploaded to a web site and displayed in a web browser such as Internet Explorer.

Creating an Executable File

WHEN USING YOUR PC, you will use executable files all the time. Each time you run Internet Explorer, MS Paint, or the calculator, you are running executable files. This is a standard formatted file that will run as soon as you access it from the menu bar or double-click on it from a folder. Within TGF2, you can create your games in this Windows format.

Creating Executables

Using the trial version of TGF2, you cannot create an executable game. We are showing you how to do it here for future reference or if you currently own the full version.

The process for converting your MFA TGF2 file to an executable is very straightforward:

1. Load the game that you wish to convert to an exe file.

2. Select File>Build>Application from the menu.

3. A dialog box will appear as shown in Figure 11.1., Type in the name of the game and then click on the Save button.

Your game has been saved, and you can now double-click on it and run it. You can see an example of the ChocoBreak game saved as an executable in the Game folder on the CD-ROM. The file is called Choco.exe.

Figure 11.1
The Save dialog box used to create an executable.

Internal and External Assets

If you create a game that uses external assets, such as images and sounds, you will need to place them with the game when you distribute them. Otherwise, these elements may not work. Items such as the active object and .wav sound files are stored internally, but other objects can be used externally, such as the Picture object and video files.

Zipping the File

AFTER YOU CREATE your executable file, you may want to place it within a zip file. A zip file can be considered a filing cabinet where you store your files. You can place a single file or many files in a zip file, and it will then be just one single file, which you can easily distribute. Zip files also have other features, notably, password protection and the ability to compress the files to make a version smaller than the original, and so easier to e-mail.

Executable Files

Some anti-virus programs and e-mail clients balk at executables sent in an e-mail. Outlook, for example, will remove the actual executable from within the e-mail so that you cannot access it.

Zip Password Security

Even though zip password security may be very useful, don't forget to make a note of the password you have used. Although it is possible to download software from the Internet to access a password from a zip file, it does require more time and effort. It's better if you just make sure you remember your password!

Zip Compression

Zip compression can make some of your files a lot smaller. This has the added benefit of any zip file you upload being smaller than the original. This can save you valuable bandwidth if you have limited download limits. Zip compression works better on some files than others, so you may find that zipping your file does not save you any space whatsoever. Zip compression does not compress executable files very well (if at all in many cases), but can be very good on graphics formats such as BMP and JPG.

Windows XP and Vista both come with a built-in zip utility. To zip a file in Windows:

1. Locate the folder where the files you want to zip are located. In the case of this example, we will use some of the book files that the author has been working on in the production of this book. You can see a folder with some files in Figure 11.2.

Figure 11.2
The folder that is being used for zipping.

2. Select the files that you want to place in a zip file. You can select a single file by clicking on it. You can select a group of files from one continuous point to another using the Shift key and highlighting all the files in a group, or you can select multiple non-contiguous files using the Ctrl key and clicking on each file individually. In this example, we have selected the Choco.exe file only, as shown in Figure 11.3.

Figure 11.3
The file that has been selected ready for zipping.

3. Right-click on the highlighted file and then, from the popup menu, select Send To > Compressed (zipped) folder. You can see this in Figure 11.4 on a Windows XP system.

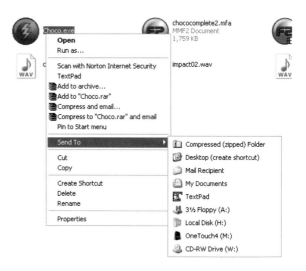

Figure 11.4
The menu option in XP to zip a file, files, or folder(s).

4. The zip utility will then compress the file and place it within a single zip file, which can be seen in Figure 11.5.

Figure 11.5
The executable file now placed in a zip file.

Selecting Files to Zip

If you are sending zip files of your games to your friends or uploading the files to the Internet, you would only need to select the executable and any external asset files, such as images. Unless you do not mind people seeing your code files, do not zip your MFA game files with your executable. This would allow anyone (if the file is on the Internet) to download your game code, and if they have the right software, they can also export images and sounds from the file.

If this were your file and it were now in a zip file, you would have it ready to e-mail or upload to the Internet. The user can download the zip, and as long as he is running XP or Vista, he will be able to extract the files to his machine and play the game. If he doesn't have XP or Vista, he can download zip utilities off the Internet. Winzip is a zip compression program, and a trial can be downloaded from www.winzip.com.

Zip File Names

The zip file that is created will be named after the last selected file, effectively, the last file placed into the zip file. We have only one file for the example we have just used, so in this case, the file is called Choco.zip.

Creating an Installer

CREATING A ZIP FILE is very useful, but it requires that users have the correct software (Vista or XP) or a zip utility. It also requires them to download the file, place it somewhere, extract the files, and then remember where they put the file and run the executable to start the game. This brings a lot of possible variables into play where the user might not be computer-literate and might have trouble running the file.

It is easier and more straightforward for the user if she can run a single executable file and install the software directly onto her computer. She would follow some simple onscreen instructions and once those are complete, an icon would be placed on the desktop or on the startup toolbar. The user doesn't have to worry about extraction or where to find the files; she can just double-click on the shortcut that has been created for her.

As a developer, you may also want to include other files, a license document to tell the user any rules that are associated with the software, provide a web link to access your web site, and a multitude of other things. Doing this in a zip file is not practical because you will have many files that the user is unlikely to access. Creating an installer fixes a number of possible issues and provides you with a way to give the user access to all manner of information as she installs the program.

An install system is built into TGF2, and although it is not as complex as some installer programs available on the market, it is built into the program and does not cost you any more than the original cost of TGF2.

Install Program

The install program in TGF2 is only useable if you have the full version. We document it here to show you how to use it should you decide to purchase the full program.

Install Creator

If you want a more powerful installation program for your games, you can use the free program called Install Creator, which is also available from Clickteam.com. The install program has an advertisement for the software at the end of the installation program, but it is very powerful and a good way of distributing your games.

To create your installer, you will need to do the following:

1. First, you need to have a game already open in TGF2, and you should have already compiled an executable game. Once you have done this, click on the application name in the Workspace properties toolbar to access the application properties.

2. You will now see the application properties. One of the options within that window is Install Settings and an Edit button as shown in Figure 11.6.

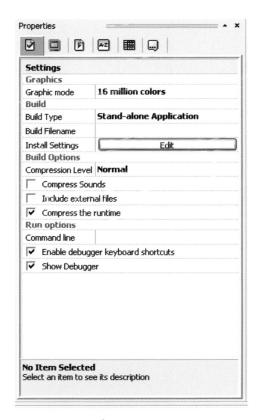

Figure 11.6
The properties of the application include an Install Settings option.

3. Click on the Edit button to access the installer program (remember this will only work in the full version).

4. You will now see an Install Settings dialog box as seen in Figure 11.7.

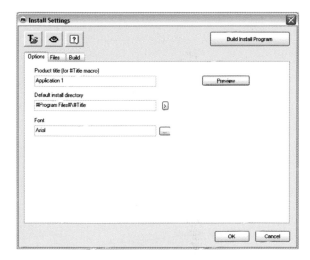

Figure 11.7
The Install Settings dialog box.

5. Type in the name of the product (game) in the area where it currently says Application1 in the image. If you have loaded a game that has a different application name, it will display it here instead (for example, ChocoBreak).

6. The default installation direction is the standard Windows installation path in Program Files. Unless you have a very good reason to do otherwise, this path is the best place to put your game files.

7. Clicking on the File tab will display which files are in the installer to be installed on the end user's PC. In Figure 11.8, the example game we have loaded into TGF2 only contains a single file called test.exe.

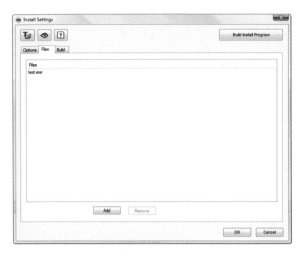

Figure 11.8
The files that the installer will place on the user's PC.

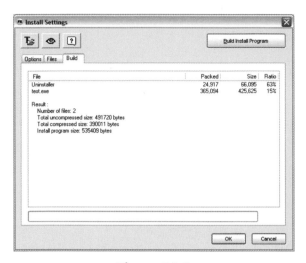

Figure 11.9
The Build installation tab.

8. On clicking the Build Install Program button, you will be provided with a dialog box asking you where to save the executable installation file. Here, you would enter your installer name, for example, Chocosetup.exe.

9. Once the installation is complete and the file is created, you can view a report on the success of the process on the Build tab. This report will also detail how much space was saved when it compressed the files and what files have been included in the installer. You can see the Build tab in Figure 11.9.

ChocoBreak Setup

On the CD-ROM that comes with this book, we have placed the installer example created using this same process for the ChocoBreak game. It is called ChocoSetup.exe and is located in the Game folder.

Web Browser Games

I F YOU HAVE A WEB PAGE or web site that you want to make more interactive, or perhaps you want to upload your games so other people can play them without downloading them, there is another build option available to TGF2. TGF2 has its own web browser plug-in called Vitalize, which allows you to place a specially formatted file onto your web site, then point to it via your web page. Users will need to download a small plug-in to play the game, but once they have downloaded the plug-in, they will be able to access any Vitalize games that you upload.

Vitalize Plug-in

The Vitalize plug-in works on many different browsers, but will only work for a Windows-based machine.

Vitalize Site

If you want to take a look at a sample web site that contains Vitalize-based games, you can visit www.madword.com. This is an arcade web site with a growing number of Vitalize-based games.

Creating Web Games

You can only create web-based games in the full version of TGF2, although you are able to download the free plug-in for TGF2 and play Vitalize games for free.

There are a number of steps for creating your game online. These can be detailed as:

▶ **Create a CCN file format. This is the format used and read by the Vitalize plug-in.**

▶ **Create or edit a web page with a link to the CCN file. You may also amend some additional information that will affect how the link will look on the page.**

▶ **Upload the CCN and HTML page you have created to a web site.**

▶ **Go to the page and test.**

Follow these steps to create your CCN game file:

1. Start up TGF2. Then click on File>Open and find the file that you want to upload as a web game. In this example, we are loading the file chococomplete3.mfa, which is located in the Game folder on the CD-ROM.

2. Click on the application name, which in the case of chococomplete3.mfa is chocobreak. This will display the application properties in the properties window. Click on the Build Type drop down menu, which is currently set to Stand-alone application, and change it to Internet Application as shown in Figure 11.10.

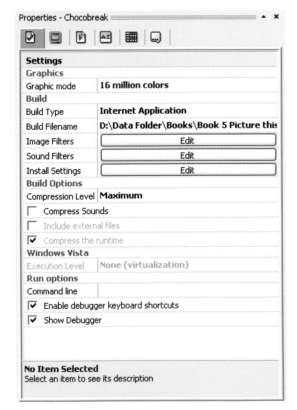

Figure 11.10
The Build Type allow you to build different types of programs.

3. Select File>Build>Application from the menu. TGF2 will then ask for the file name of the CCN file. In this case, we saved it as Choco.ccn.

By placing this code within your HTML file and changing a few items, you can quickly get a game displayed on a web page. This HTML page can be viewed from your machine, on a CD-ROM, or on a web site.

▶ **Width:** This is the width of your game.

▶ **Height:** This is the height of the game.

▶ **Codebase:** This is the page location of the Vitalize plug-in. When the page loads, it will check to determine whether Vitalize is installed. If not, it will start the plug-in installation. There is a version number on the end of this line, and the program you created in TGF2 will check to see if you're running the latest plug-in. If you have an older version, it will ask you to update. This version code is for Internet Explorer only.

▶ **PARAM NAME="URL":** This is the location of the CCN game. You can place the game in the same folder as the HTML file or in another location.

▶ **Checkversion:** This will check the version of the plug-in installed and update the user's version if it's not up-to-date. This is used for Firefox, Netscape, and Opera.

▶ **WIDTH/HEIGHT:** Enter additional width and height information for non-Internet Explorer browsers.

Create a standard web page, and within the <body> and </body> tag of your HTML file, you will need to insert a specific set of code as shown:

Vitalize Code

```
<OBJECT ID="Vitalize1" WIDTH=320 HEIGHT=200 type="application/x-cnc"

CLASSID="CLSID:EB6D7E70-AAA9-40D9-BA05-F214089F2275"

CODEBASE="http://www.clickteam.com/vitalize4/vitalize.cab#Version=4,0,248,1">

<PARAM NAME="URL" VALUE="yourapp.ccn">

<EMBED TYPE="application/x-cnc"

SRC="yourapp.ccn"

checkversion="4,0,248,1"

PLUGINSPAGE="http://www.clickteam.com/vitalize4/download.html"

WIDTH=320

HEIGHT=200>

</EMBED>

</OBJECT>
```

We have placed the game ChocoBreak within a web page on the CD. This will show you how to place the game on a page. When running the game offline, you will be given a security warning about running the CCN file. This is normal, and all programs that are plug-ins on a web page will do this when you are not online.

You can find the web page called Vitalize.html located in the Game folder on the CD-ROM that accompanies this book. You may also notice that the CCN file is located in the same folder.

If you try to run this game offline, you will not be able to access the Vitalize plug-in. You can install this from the CD-ROM rather than the Internet; the setup file is located in the Demos folder and is called instvtz4.exe.

Battle Lords

Play

Options

Quit

Testing Your
Games

I N CHAPTER 11 WE DISCUSSED HOW you could compile, package, and distribute your games. You may spend a lot of time making your games, but before you distribute them you will need to test them to ensure they don't contain any bugs. These bugs may be errors with your code (events) or a mistake in the way you designed your game. Either way, it is always a good idea to take a look at your program from a gamer's perspective rather than from a programmer's view to ensure that the game is working correctly before you distribute it.

Although we could have put this chapter on testing your games before Chapter 11, "Distribution," we chose to reverse the order for a very good reason. The best way to test your game is to create it as if it were ready to be installed, downloaded, or extracted by the user, so you need to understand how to do that before you can test it.

By testing your game precisely as the user would receive the game, you will have more chances of finding any problems. This will help solve distribution errors as well as bugs within your game.

Lovely Bugs

UNFORTUNATELY, NO MATTER how hard we try to make the perfect game, there will always be some issue with it. As a games programmer, you might spend a lot of time making your games and because so much effort and focus are placed upon creating the game, it is very common to miss bugs or issues that may irritate the end user.

These bugs can range from simple spelling mistakes to game crashes that can make the game unplayable. The longer you have spent on making your game, the more acute this issue becomes. The longer the development time, the more chance that you will want to rush the final stage of your game and get it released as quickly as possible. Beware of trying to rush your game just to get it finished and released. A few simple checks can really make a difference in the final quality of your game. You might only need to spend 5 or 10 minutes or a couple of hours checking your spelling, but in the long run, it will improve what users think of your game.

The Spelling Bee Bug

You might think that simple bugs, such as spelling mistakes, can be ignored because your priority is getting your game released. Do not underestimate how much you can improve the quality of your game by spending a few hours checking spelling and grammar.

Testing Names

WHEN YOUR GAME IS in the process of being made, you will go through a number of stages of the product's life cycle. When you reach different stages of development, you will give the product a different name/classification. This helps you understand where the game currently is with regards to completeness, and, if you are using any testers, this will help them understand what they need to be doing to help you test.

▶ **General Bug Fixing or Pre-Alpha:** When you are creating your game, you will also test to see if it works. This is just to confirm that you have completed that section of code and then can move on to the next part of the program. There may also be issues with the look and feel and general stability. All of this will be done while you are programming the main part of the game, but you will not be going out of your way to find problems.

▶ **Alpha Version:** When the product is in a suitable condition and a lot of the functionality has been implemented, you can say that your product is at version alpha. This means that it could still be unstable, but it is in a state where a lot of the options are functional (though not all), and it has the general look and feel of the final product. The product may still have some major bugs and issues, but this is the first version that is considered

suitable enough to show to people as the work in progress (even if you are a hobbyist creator). The alpha is used to get feedback on how the product sticks together and if the interface works well enough. This is the final stage of development before the product will be locked down with regards to features and its look and feel. At the alpha stage, you could continue adding new features and never actually release a product because it could always be added to. The end of the alpha stage is an indication of the beginning of the final program and its functionality.

▶ **Beta:** At the end of the alpha process, you may have received comments about how the product looks and whether the interface works well. Once you are satisfied that you have taken the comments on board and have made final decisions about the interface (and made those changes to the product), then you enter the beta stage. The beta stage is where the product is fully locked down with regards to functionality, look, and feel. This stage means that all that needs to be done is the removal of any bugs within the program. You can start to give this version to your testers, who will then try and locate any problems within the game. Beta testers could be a group of friends or anyone who has downloaded the game from your web site and who replies to you with comments.

▶ **Post Release:** Once the product has been released, there will be people using the game on configurations that you may not have expected or ways that even the beta testers didn't pick up. There are generally bugs to be fixed once the product is available to a larger number of people.

Testing One, Two, Three

Different users and different companies have different testing policies. A game maker who is making games for fun at home has a totally different experience than a large games company testing games that will run on a games console. If you are making games on your own, you might decide to just wait until you have made your game before you begin to test it. Larger organizations might have teams of testers ready to test the game at different stages. You can pick or choose whichever methods that you feel are most useful to you to help you make your game better.

Using Testers

Beta testers are an essential resource for finding bugs within your games. Game developers who have been working on a product for a while will find it harder to find bugs because they are so used to the product. A new user to a product tries things that the developer just wouldn't think about and so can be a great asset for finding those bugs the developer didn't even know about.

The Debugger

WHEN YOU NEED TO test your games, there is a debugger tool within TGF2 that can help you search out problems quickly and easily. You may have noticed this tool before because it appears every time you run a TGF2 game within the editor. The debugger is very much like other debuggers for other programming languages and offers lots of nice little features to make the developer's life much easier. Every program you make contains data information, for example, the current number of lives the player has or the location of the spaceship on the screen. All of this information is essential if you wish to fix issues with your program. The new debugger allows you to get access to all of these details so you can spend more time developing your programs rather than bug finding.

Starting the Debugger

To make the debugger start, you will need to have a program running within TGF2. Once you have opened up one of your games, if you run the frame or the whole game, then the debugger will appear in the top left corner, as shown in Figure 12.1.

Figure 12.2 gives you a closer look at what the debugger bar contains.

Figure 12.1
The debugger open and ready to use.

Figure 12.2
A close-up of the debugger bar.

Debugger

The debugger will appear when you run the frame or application even if there is no content.

Memory and Objects

The debugger contains a text bar, which displays the number of objects and the memory that the current frame is using. You can get a good idea of the performance of each frame by making a note of the numbers displayed here.

There are a number of buttons and functionality that you can access:

▶ If you click on the plus (+) sign on the right side of the debugger bar, it will expand the amount of information that you will be able to see. All options and program data can now be viewed. Within the whole program (each frame, object, etc.) is specific information, such as location on the screen, screen size, current counter values, and string details. The expanded debugger can be seen in Figure 12.3. To collapse it back, click on the minus (−) sign that replaced the plus sign when you expanded the contents.

▶ The first button on the debugger bar (the line with the left pointing arrow) signifies that the program will start from the beginning of the frame once clicked. This is very useful if you are trying to track a bug and want to watch what is being changed (something we will detail shortly); you can keep repeating the process until you have found the problem.

▶ The square icon on the debugger bar is the stop button. This stops the frame and program from running, and it will also close the running game and the debugger.

▶ The third icon is the pause button, which will pause your program (nothing will happen on the game's playfield) until you press play to start it back up. This will allow you to get to a specific point in the program and then check the result of the current data being stored by TGF2.

▶ The fourth icon from the left looks like a grayed-out right pointing arrow. In fact, this is the Next Step button, which allows you to step through you game code a line at a time. To use this function, you will need to pause the program first using the pause button mentioned above. This is a very useful option if you want to see slowly what changes are made to your program (otherwise, things can happen very quickly and you might miss them).

▶ The fifth icon is the play button; once you have paused the program, you would use this to start it back at real time (playing at normal speed).

► The display in the middle of the debugger bar shows two bits of useful information: first, how many objects are being used in the current frame, and second, the amount of bytes for the total memory used by the application.

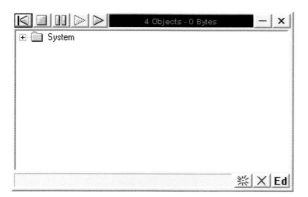

Figure 12.3
The debugger expanded to reveal more information.

Within the expanded debugger you will see the system node; by clicking on this, you can display the default information that is available in all applications. This can be seen in Figure 12.3.

Expanding the System folder, as shown in Figure 12.4, will give you all standard game information. Frame number is the current frame that is running within the game. The time is the actual amount of time that frame has been running (it is very important to remember that the time is reset between frames). You also have two additional expandable folders, which display all of the global values and global strings being used within the program. At the bottom right of the expanded debugger, you will see three additional buttons that you can use to add and remove additional items. The first icon is to add additional items; the second is to delete any items (if you only have System to begin with, it will delete that group); and finally, you will have an edit button, which is displayed as three dots and is used when you wish to edit specific data entries.

Figure 12.4
Basic information that is stored in the debugger.

Frame and Time

When you move between frames in your
game, the debugger will update the frame
number and reset the timer.

Adding Items to the Debugger

You will want to add an item to the debugger so
that you can watch it and see what happens to it
when your game is running.

1. Click on the New application button to
   create a new game file.

2. Double-click on the text "Frame 1" in the
   Workspace toolbar to access the Frame
   Editor.

3. Right-click on the blank frame and select
   Insert Object. Choose the Lives object and
   click on OK; then click on the frame to place
   the object.

4. Run the game by pressing the "run application" button on the toolbar. This will start
   the game and open up the debugger.

5. Click on the + sign on the debugger to
   expand it.

6. Click on the first of the three buttons
   (the Add object button) in the bottom right
   corner of the expanded debugger.

7. Whenever you have a frame with different
   objects, when you click on add, you will see
   a sct of folders that you can expand. In this
   case, you have already added a Lives object,
   and you can expand this folder to see the any
   Lives objects within it as shown in Figure 12.5.

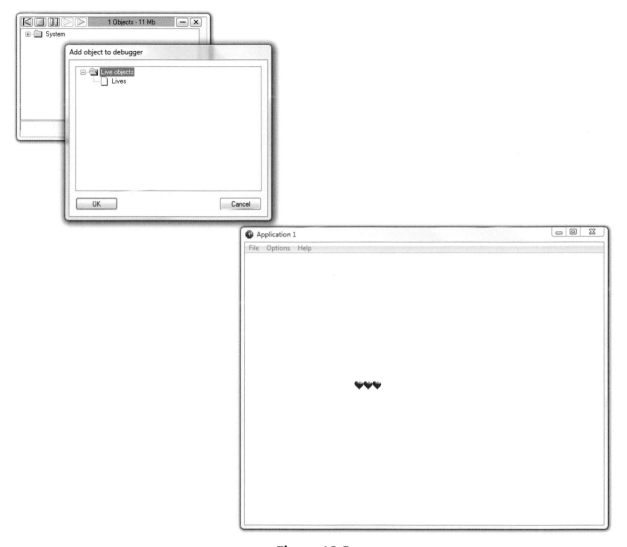

Figure 12.5
The Lives object folder with the Lives item within it.

8. Make sure the folder is expanded and select the Lives object; then click on OK.

9. Now that you have added the object, you can see its properties in the debugger, with information about its screen location, width and height, any movement that has been assigned, and any specific object information. In this case, the number of lives equals 3. This is the default setting of this object. You can see this information in Figure 12.6.

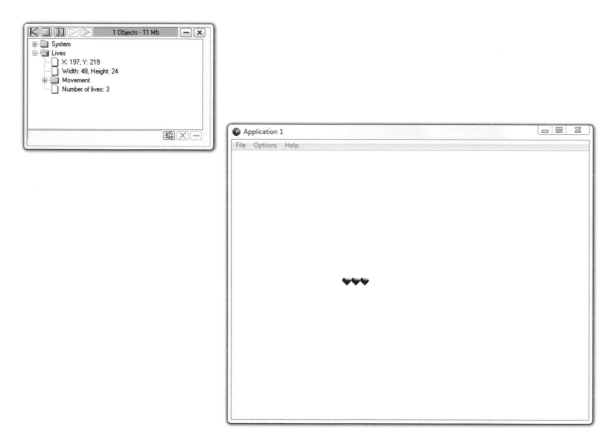

Figure 12.6
The information of the Lives object now that it has been added to the debugger.

Object Folders

In a frame you might have multiple objects of the same type; in this case, you might have more than one Lives object. These are displayed in the same folder for neatness.

Each Frame's Objects

It is important to note that for each frame, you will need to set up the objects that you want to watch. Once you move frames, the debugger resets the items within its list to just the original System folder. This is because each frame will have different objects allocated to them, so it needs to do this to refresh the list. You will need to add any objects you want to watch in each frame.

Editing Object Properties

Sometimes within your game you may want to change the value of an item to see what effect it might have on your game. You can use the Edit object button to set a particular value to an object. In this case, we are using the simple example file we just created with the Lives object onscreen.

1. Run the game that you want to test (in this case, it is the single Lives object on frame 1). Expand the debugger by clicking on the + button.

2. Ensure that the Lives object is added to the debugger using the Add object button.

3. Expand the Lives folder so that you can see the item "Number of lives:3".

4. You can either double-click on that item or single-click on the item and click on the Edit button.

5. When you are in edit mode, a small dialog box will appear allowing you to edit the contents. Once you have changed the content (typed in another value), you can click on OK to save this information back to the program.

6. You can see that if you haven't paused the game before you change the value, the value will automatically update. If you change the lives to 2, the number of heart graphics on the frame also changes to 2.

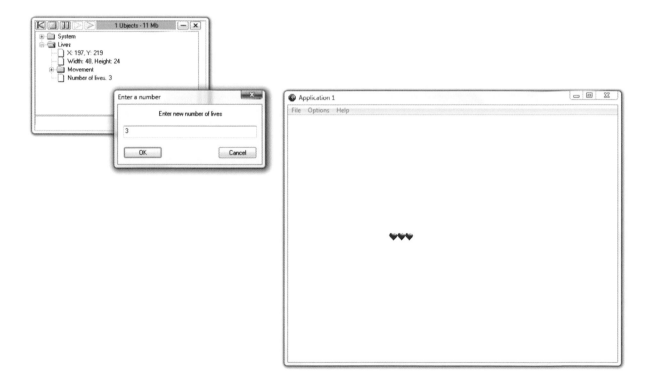

Figure 12.7
The Edit box where you can change the information and save it back into the program.

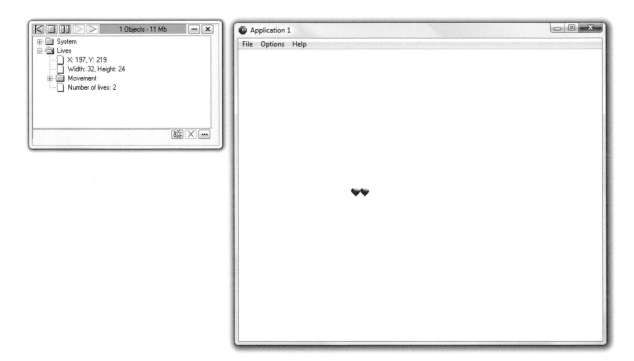

Figure 12.8
The updated frame which reflects the changes made to the debugger dialog box.

Editing Objects Information

Changing any data when running the debugger is only a temporary change. In this example, we amended the number of lives. Once the program has finished and we run it again, any amended data will be reset back to its original settings.

This chapter presented the basics of using the debugger. As you create larger games, you will find yourself using this program more and more to help you find any programming issues with your game. It is very useful and can save you lots of time and effort trying to find those difficult bugs that you couldn't see in the Event Editor. It's a great little tool that you should consider looking at if you start to get stuck with your game and you are not sure why it's not doing what you have told it to do.

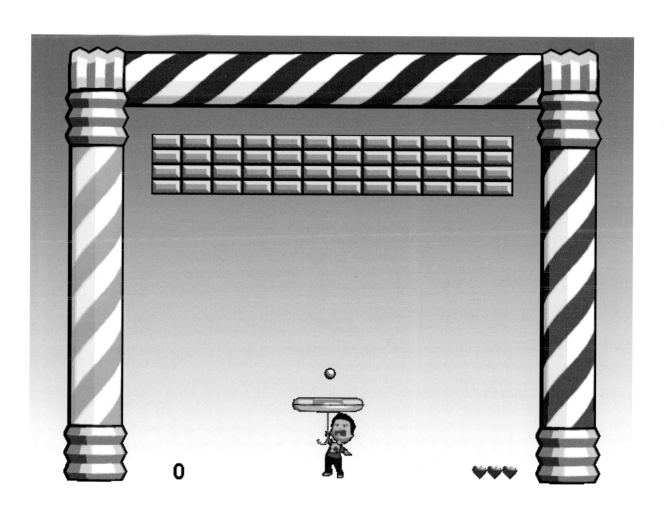

A

Keyboard
Shortcuts

KEYBOARD SHORTCUTS ALLOW YOU to use certain key combinations to do things quicker rather than finding items within the menu system. Within TGF2 there is a default set of shortcut commands, but you can also amend them to suit your own requirements. Over time, you may find that you are duplicating certain menu combinations when you are developing your games; by setting up your own keyboard shortcuts, you will be able to work faster and more efficiently. The other option you have is not to change the defaults but to make a list of all the important key combinations that you use for future reference.

To view the default keyboard preferences:

1. Start TGF2, and go to the menu bar at the top of the program.

2. Select the Tools option.

3. Select the Keyboard Shortcuts option.

The keyboard shortcuts dialog box will load, as shown in Figure A.1.

Some default key combinations can be seen in Table A.1.

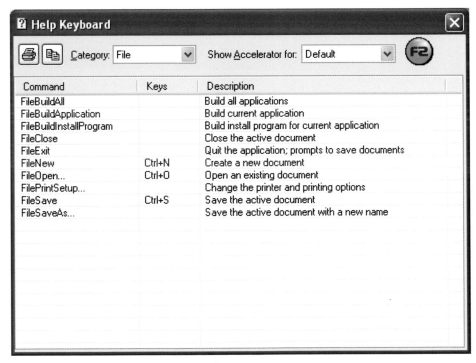

Figure A.1
Keyboard shortcut list dialog box.

Table A.1 Common Key Combinations and Shortcut Keys

Action	Key Combination or Shortcut Keys	Details
Copy	Ctrl+C	Copy the selection and put it on the clipboard
Cut	Ctrl+X	Cut the selection and put it on the clipboard
Delete	Delete	Delete the selected object
Enlarge canvas	Ctrl+W	Enlarge the canvas of the picture
Event Editor	Ctrl+E	Open the Event Editor window
Events list editor	Ctrl+L	Open event list window
Find	Ctrl+F	Find the specified text
Frame Editor	Ctrl+M	Open Frame Editor window
Help	Shift+F1	Display help for clicked on buttons, menus, and windows
New	Ctrl+N	Create a new document
Open	Ctrl+O	Open an existing document
Paste	Ctrl+V	Insert clipboard contents
Play	F5	Play the current frame from the current position
Print	Ctrl+P	Print the active document
Redo	Ctrl+Y	Redo the previously undone action
Run Application	F8	Run the current application
Run Frame	F7	Run the current frame
Save	Ctrl+S	Save the active document
Select All	Ctrl+A	Select the entire document
Storyboard Editor	Ctrl+B	Open storyboard window
Undo	Ctrl+Z	Undo the last action
Zoom in	F2	Zoom the current window inwards
Zoom out	F3	Zoom the current window outwards
Zoom to fit	F4	Set the zoom factor of the current window to obtain a complete display

B

Bibliography

WE HOPE YOU HAVE ENJOYED your experience of video game creation. If you want to take your game creating skills to the next level, there are a number of other books written by Jason Darby that can help you in your game creating goals.

Make Amazing Games in Minutes

MANY GAME ENTHUSIASTS have aspirations to create their own games but don't know where to start. *Make Amazing Games in Minutes* introduces the game creation process to the aspiring game developer with no experience or programming ability. Taking the reader step-by-step through the various stages of developing a game and using the popular "drag-and-drop" game creation software included on the CD-ROM, this book will help the reader build his very own games. Using the tutorials and step-by-step methods, the reader will complete a fully playable retro game, as well as platform, bat and ball, and side-scrolling shoot 'em up games. Other chapters cover more complex game features such as adding effects and scoreboards, porting the game onto the web, and installation script building. This must-have book is the essential resource for anyone interested in learning game creation and the retro game style.

Make Amazing Games in Minutes
ISBN: 1-58450-407-2

Power User's Guide to Windows Development

ICROSOFT WINDOWS is the most popular operating system in the world. Millions of computers are shipped every year with it as the OS, making Windows the platform of choice for developers. And because of its widespread use, there are numerous programming languages that can be used to create applications that will work with Windows. But you don't have to be a programmer to develop practical, fun, and interesting applications with Windows. Many people have learned how to harness the power of Windows to make their own tools, and the *Power User's Guide to Windows Development* will teach you how to create your own without knowing how to program! Written for power Windows users, web developers, and beginning programmers who want to go beyond the basic functional uses of Windows but who aren't programmers, this book is a complete guide to making your own games, music players, CD-ROM menus, screensavers, movie players, advertising materials, and more. Using a free trial version of Multimedia Fusion 2 Developer (Clickteam), you'll learn how to develop your own tools in Windows. A variety of fun projects are used throughout the book to get you developing practical applications quickly. Beginning with basic screensavers, you'll progress through edutainment tools, interactive tutorials, games, CD-ROM menus, graphic creation, videos, music, and networking tools. So, if you want to make your own applications to use on Windows, *Power User's Guide to Windows Development* will teach you everything you need to know—no programming required!

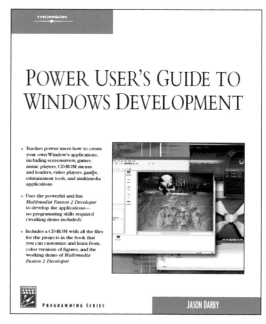

Power User's Guide to Windows Development
ISBN: 1-58450-518-4

Awesome Game Creation: No Programming Required, Third Edition

THIS IS ONE OF THE FIRST BOOKS Charles River Media published in game development, and it has been very successful. There are thousands more game players today than there were in 2000 and many of these players want to know how to make their own games. Most of these people are not programmers, however, so they need a non-programming way to learn and that's why this book works so well! *Awesome Game Creation: No Programming Required,* Third Edition teaches game enthusiasts and aspiring developers how to create their own computer games without programming skills. It teaches how the whole game design process works, beginning with an overview of how to design a game, and moving through the creation process from the basic building blocks to sound, music, and graphics. Throughout the book, you'll learn how to create a variety of games, including a 2D dragon flying game, first person shooter, space shoot 'em up, and more. To make sure you're able to follow along easily, each game is created through step-by-step tutorials that use "drag-and-drop" game engines. You'll learn how to make and modify your own interactive 2D and 3D computer games. And, you'll learn how to use a variety of development tools, including The Games Factory 2 (latest version), GameMaker, and FPS Creator (new to this edition). This is a great way to learn the basics of game design and creation without having to learn how to program!

Awesome Game Creation: No Programming Required, Third Edition
ISBN: 1-58450-534-6

Game Creation for Teens

L EARN HOW TO CREATE your very own video games to play and share with friends! *Game Creation for Teens* teaches beginners how to build games using The Games Factory 2, a simple drag-and-drop software. No previous programming or game development experience is required to get started, and the technology and software used in the book will show readers how to create a variety of games. Using the hands-on tutorials presented in the book, aspiring game developers will create three games that incorporate graphics, sound and music, objects, and more, and even discover how to test and fix their games.

Game Creation for Teens
ISBN: 1-59863-500X

Picture Yourself Creating Video Games

T HE BOOK YOU NOW HOLD in your hands, *Picture Yourself Creating Video Games,* teaches amateur game creators how to make their very own games, with no programming skills or prior experience required! The easy to follow, step-by-step instructions use a drag-and-drop software, the Games Factory 2, to show readers everything they need to create their own video games for fun. Readers will learn simple programming terms, storyboarding techniques, and basic game creation skills. And the Games Factory 2 provides all the components they need to create games including heroes, monsters, sound, and music.

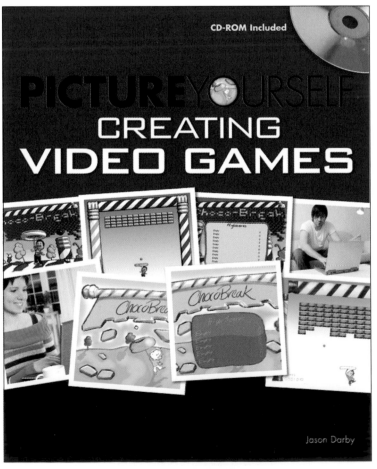

Picture Yourself Creating Video Games
ISBN: 1-59863-551-4

Going to War: Creating Computer War Games

COMING SOON!

Have you ever wanted to recreate a famous battle from history or imagined a battle on a distant planet? If you love to play tabletop war games or strategy computer games, now is the chance to make your own computer war games. This book gives you all you need to know to make your own computer war games, including movement, weather effects, and terrain issues. Using an easy-to-use game creation program, you will be making games rather than worrying about how to code, and in no time, you will be recreating your own ideas and battles. ISBN: 1-59863-566-2

Index

License Agreement/Notice of Limited Warranty

By opening the sealed disc container in this book, you agree to the following terms and conditions. If, upon reading the following license agreement and notice of limited warranty, you cannot agree to the terms and conditions set forth, return the unused book with unopened disc to the place where you purchased it for a refund.

License:

The enclosed software is copyrighted by the copyright holder(s) indicated on the software disc. You are licensed to copy the software onto a single computer for use by a single user and to a backup disc. You may not reproduce, make copies, or distribute copies or rent or lease the software in whole or in part, except with written permission of the copyright holder(s). You may transfer the enclosed disc only together with this license, and only if you destroy all other copies of the software and the transferee agrees to the terms of the license. You may not decompile, reverse assemble, or reverse engineer the software.

Notice of Limited Warranty:

The enclosed disc is warranted by Course Technology to be free of physical defects in materials and workmanship for a period of sixty (60) days from end user's purchase of the book/disc combination. During the sixty-day term of the limited warranty, Course Technology will provide a replacement disc upon the return of a defective disc.

Limited Liability:

THE SOLE REMEDY FOR BREACH OF THIS LIMITED WARRANTY SHALL CONSIST ENTIRELY OF REPLACEMENT OF THE DEFECTIVE DISC. IN NO EVENT SHALL COURSE TECHNOLOGY OR THE AUTHOR BE LIABLE FOR ANY OTHER DAMAGES, INCLUDING LOSS OR CORRUPTION OF DATA, CHANGES IN THE FUNCTIONAL CHARACTERISTICS OF THE HARDWARE OR OPERATING SYSTEM, DELETERIOUS INTERACTION WITH OTHER SOFTWARE, OR ANY OTHER SPECIAL, INCIDENTAL, OR CONSEQUENTIAL DAMAGES THAT MAY ARISE, EVEN IF COURSE TECHNOLOGY AND/OR THE AUTHOR HAS PREVIOUSLY BEEN NOTIFIED THAT THE POSSIBILITY OF SUCH DAMAGES EXISTS.

Disclaimer of Warranties:

COURSE TECHNOLOGY AND THE AUTHOR SPECIFICALLY DISCLAIM ANY AND ALL OTHER WARRANTIES, EITHER EXPRESS OR IMPLIED, INCLUDING WARRANTIES OF MERCHANTABILITY, SUITABILITY TO A PARTICULAR TASK OR PURPOSE, OR FREEDOM FROM ERRORS. SOME STATES DO NOT ALLOW FOR EXCLUSION OF IMPLIED WARRANTIES OR LIMITATION OF INCIDENTAL OR CONSEQUENTIAL DAMAGES, SO THESE LIMITATIONS MIGHT NOT APPLY TO YOU.

Other:

This Agreement is governed by the laws of the State of Massachusetts without regard to choice of law principles. The United Convention of Contracts for the International Sale of Goods is specifically disclaimed. This Agreement constitutes the entire agreement between you and Course Technology regarding use of the software.